I0198217

WAIT...WHAT?

Biblical Teachings Worth Repeating

by
Kelly Brady

EQUIP Publishing

WAIT...WHAT?
Biblical Teachings Worth Repeating

Copyright @ 2022 by Kelly Brady
Second Edition. Printed in the U.S.A., Published by EQUIP

All rights reserved. No part of this publication may be reproduced, stored, or transmitted in any form by any means, electronic, mechanical, photocopy, recording, or otherwise, without prior written permission by the author.

All Scripture quotations, unless otherwise indicated, are taken from the HOLY BIBLE, NEW INTERNATIONAL VERSION®. Copyright © 1973, 1978, 1984 by International Bible Society. Used by permission of Zondervan. All rights reserved.

Scripture marked NASB are taken from the New American Standard Bible®, Copyright © 1960, 1962, 1963, 1968, 1971, 1972, 1973, 1975, 1977, 1995 by the Lockman Foundation. Used by permission.

Scripture marked ESV are from the Holy Bible, English Standard Version, copyright © 2001 by Crossway, a publishing ministry of Good New Publishers. Used by permission. All rights reserved.

Scripture quotations marked (NLT) are taken from the Holy Bible, New Living Translation, copyright © 1996, 2004, 2007 by Tyndale House Foundation. Used by permission of Tyndale House Publishers, Inc., Carol Stream, Illinois 60188. All rights reserved.

ISBN 13: 978-0-692-14810-5   ISBN 10: 0-692-14810-8

Also by Dr. Kelly Brady

FOLLOWING JESUS
Defining Discipleship in the 21st Century

DRIVE THRU THEOLOGY
A guide to the Bible's teaching for those on the go

SHEPHERDING
The Elder Notebook of
Glen Ellyn Bible Church

To my mom,

Theresa Brady

who has always encouraged
my spiritual leadership.

TABLE OF CONTENTS

To equip his people for works of service,
so that the body of Christ may be built up.
Ephesians 4:12 (NIV)

Introduction

Jesus described himself as the Good Shepherd and those who follow him as his sheep (John 10:11). Being compared to sheep is not flattering. There are stories, for example, of sheep walking into an open fire! There are also stories of sheep being stuck on their back, unable to right themselves. It's called being "cast." It can happen when sheep grow too fat, or when their wool is too heavy. The short of it is that sheep can be too weak to care for themselves and too stubborn to change course, a deadly combination. Yet, I must be honest. I certainly find within myself a lot of sheep-like tendencies.

Jesus is the Good Shepherd, but he also gifts and calls some sheep to help him in the work of shepherding (Ephesians 4:11-12). That's my passion. I love helping other sheep follow the Good Shepherd. Toward that end, this book is a collection of sermon excerpts from the last couple decades, teachings that I've offered to those I shepherd. The title, "Wait...What?" came from my teenage children, who daily remind me of the value of repeating important messages.

The chapters are short. Most are less than four pages in length and can be read in under 12 minutes. Each chapter is headed by a verse. Make sure to open your Bible and read each verse in context to get the full impact of the teaching. Finally, *Going Deeper* discussion questions are also included with each chapter. These questions are designed to help the reader apply the teaching to their life, as well as facilitate discussion with others.

Children of God

Truly, I say to you, unless you turn and become like children,
you will never enter the Kingdom of heaven.
Matthew 18:3 (ESV)

There is not another species on the planet that has a longer stage of functional "dependence" than humans. Functional "*in*dependence" is marked by the ability to do things like walk, talk, and feed oneself. This means that among all species of animals, humans are some of the most helpless at birth and it takes us longer than any other species to become independent. For example, compare humans with deer or horses. When these animals are born, they quickly become independent, as they can almost immediately stand and are soon able to feed themselves. While humans don't walk, talk, or feed themselves for years! Yet, as adults we are the highest functioning species on the planet. Scientists call these two different types of babies *altricial* and *precocial*. Altricial babies are born helpless. Their brains are not fully developed, and they are completely dependent on others at birth. This is the human experience. Precocial babies, are near fully functional at birth.

What might we learn spiritually from the long period of functional dependence for humans during childhood? I ask because childhood is used in Scripture to describe the nature of our relationship with God. For example, Jesus said that we "must be born again" (John 3:3). In other words, it's not enough to simply understand the gospel, we must be born into it like children are born into the world biologically helpless and dependent. Jesus is saying that there is an altricial experience that we must all have if we are to be related to God. How does this happen? Matthew recorded Jesus' explanation writing:

> At that time the disciples came to Jesus, saying, "Who is the greatest in the kingdom of heaven?" And calling to him a child, he put him in the midst of them and said, "Truly, I say to you, unless you turn and become like children, you will never enter the kingdom of heaven. Whoever humbles himself like this child is the greatest in the kingdom of heaven." Matthew 18:1-4 (ESV)

Children are humble in their utter dependence upon their parents. There was a point in all our lives when our parents clothed us, fed us, and provided shelter for us. In much the same way, Scripture teaches that we must "turn," admitting our complete dependence upon God for salvation. We are children spiritually as we cry out to God for help with our sin. That's what children do. They cry out for their needs to be met.

Scripture teaches that we are dead in our sin, unable to provide life for ourselves, but that God in his grace offers us life. Rather than asserting our power and authority like adults so often do, we are to admit our need for God's care by placing our faith in Jesus' death for the forgiveness of sin and Jesus' resurrection for the power to live a God honoring life. If you have never cried out to God in a childlike, dependent, and humble fashion you can do that at any time.

Talk to God, as you would talk with anyone, expressing your desire to have forgiveness of sin and life through faith in Jesus. After all, what if humans have such a long stage of functional "dependence" to provide a living example of the dependence required to enter the kingdom?

Going Deeper Questions

1. How are children dependent on their parents in ways similar to the dependence we are to have upon God?

   _____

   _____

   _____

   _____

2. What barriers exist for people becoming children of God?

   _____

   _____

   _____

3. How can you become even more childlike in your dependence upon God?

   _____

   _____

   _____

   _____

Childlike, Not Childish

When I became a man, I gave up childish ways.
1 Corinthians 13:11 (ESV)

Every metaphor has its limits. Meaning, you can always stretch an example too far. For that reason, it's important to understand that there is a difference between being childlike in our faith and being childish as a person of faith. Make no mistake. While we are to be childlike in our dependence upon God for salvation, God would not have us be childish in the way we live. For example, children are fairly easily fooled. They tend to accept things without question, often being drawn into falsehood. While God would have us live in a posture of humble dependence upon him for salvation, he would not have us to be easily duped. While childlike innocence with regard to sin is laudable, naiveté is not, and in Paul's letter to the Ephesians, he points out the value of maturity. He wrote:

> We are no longer to be children, tossed here and there by waves and carried about by every wind of doctrine, by the trickery of men, by craftiness in deceitful scheming. Ephesians 4:14 (NASB)

God wants us to enjoy the blessings of stability brought by maturity in the faith. God doesn't want us to be childishly tossed by every new teaching that comes our way, like a boat is tossed by the sea. Therefore, being childlike in our dependence on God does not mean being simple-minded.

Children are also often childish in their selfishness. Children can be willful, self-absorbed, and self-interested. Obviously, God does not want us to emulate children in this way. God wants us to be done with "childish ways" (1 Corinthians 13:11). God wants us to grow up and demonstrate the maturity needed to care for others and bear one another's burdens.

How does this happen? Being a child of God, without being childish is realized as we are obedient to follow Jesus' teachings and example, particularly his example of selfless sacrifice. Too often it seems that Christians have not simply been saved by grace, but that we have been paralyzed by it, believing that nothing is expected of those whom God has redeemed. Interestingly though, Jesus said:

> Do not think that I have come to abolish the Law
> or the Prophets; I have not come to abolish them
> but to fulfill them. Matthew 5:17 (NIV)

The word "fulfill" in this verse means literally "to give full meaning." In other words, we see in the character, conduct and concerns of Jesus a living demonstration of God's holiness as reflected in the law. We live as children of God, without being childish, as we are obedient to follow Jesus' law-keeping example. And the good news is the God has provided us a means for obedience as his children. He has given us his Spirit (Galatians 4:6-7). The same Spirit that descended upon Jesus at his baptism, dwells in those who have been born again as God's children.

This means the same Spirit who enabled Jesus to fully meet the righteous requirements of the law, will enable Christians to follow Jesus' example. Although much in this world encourages childishness, the reality is that God has called us to be holy and enabled us to pursue holiness by his Spirit (Ephesians 1:4, 1 Peter 1:15-16).

Going Deeper Questions

1. There is a tension between being childlike in our faith and childish as a person of faith. Why does this tension exist?

   _____

   _____

   _____

   _____

2. How have you matured in your faith over the last few years?

   _____

   _____

   _____

   _____

3. What barriers exist to you going on toward maturity in the faith?

   _____

   _____

   _____

   _____

   _____

Sheep-like Tendencies

The Lord is my shepherd.
Psalm 23:1

Ever follow your appetites too far? Sheep do it all the time. Head down, with their eyes on the ground and minds completely engrossed in filling their bellies they wander through a pasture eating, until they are completely separated from the flock, lost and all alone. So strong is their appetite that sheep will not lie down and rest unless they feel sure that ample food is available. They continue in search of food, even if it means driving themselves to exhaustion, and they must be *made* to lie down, as the Psalmist described (Psalm 23:2).

Discontentedness is also a problem for sheep. It's not just that they are driven by their appetite, they often also want what they don't need. With easy access to a pasture full of grass, they reach for grass on the other side of a fence or among thorns and get hung up. Ever make poor relational decisions, reaching for something off limits, only to get hung-up emotionally, entangled in sin, and unable to fully enjoy what was easily within reach?

Physical weakness is a problem for sheep too. In fact, their strong appetites and discontented dispositions might not be such a problem if they were not also uniquely weak physically. For example, because of their short legs and heavy wool, they must be very careful where they lie down. If they aren't paying close attention, they can roll to their side and wind up unable to get back on their feet. It's called being "cast."

Thrashing around helplessly on their side, they soon find themselves upside down, completely on their backs. In this position, the blood begins to leave their legs, which then grow numb and they eventually become completely immobile. If the weather is hot, they may last only a couple of hours. If the weather is cool, they may last a couple of days. Ever get careless and find yourself helpless and in need of rescue?

Perhaps the greatest threat to sheep though is their fear. Sheep are easily spooked, and when that happens they become confused, which leads to their making poor decisions. Ever allow fear to drive you into self-sabotaging behavior? There are countless tales of sheep plunging off steep cliffs, *together* no less, an entire herd running to their death out of fear and in confusion. So fearful and prone to confusion are sheep that they will not drink from rushing water. Can you imagine? Their fear of rushing water can prevent them from getting the hydration they need to survive. For sheep to drink from water it must be calm, quiet waters.

With all our sheep-like tendencies in mind, Jesus said of himself, "I am the good shepherd" (John 10:11-16), and all of the benefits listed in Psalm 23 (i.e., the green pastures, the quiet waters, the paths of righteousness, and the experience of peace even in the place of darkest fear) become ours when we admit our sheep-like tendencies.

What does Jesus' "goodness" as our shepherd mean for us? It means that he laid down his life for us so that we may be forgiven (Isaiah 53:6). But it is not simply salvation from our sin that the Good Shepherd made possible through his death on the cross.

It's true that we are saved *from* the consequences of our sin through faith in Jesus, but we are also saved *to* something. We are saved to a relationship with our Creator. This is a staggering reality. Jesus knows our past with its failures and its hurts. He knows our present, including our wounds and weaknesses. He knows our future, including our fears, and he still loves us and offered himself for us nonetheless. And we can know him too. This is a relationship in the fullest sense of the word. As our good shepherd, we can know his ways and his will for our lives. We can know

> *All of the benefits listed in Psalm 23 become ours when we admit our sheep-like tendencies.*

his power and provision, as he meets our needs. We can know his presence too. As he speaks to us, we hear his voice.

Unfortunately, many are tempted to pretend that they don't have sheep-like tendencies. But the only animal that humanity is compared with in Scripture is sheep. I'd like to have been compared to a cheetah, or a lion, or a bear, or a bull, or an elephant. But that's not the case, and the truth is that my appetites lead me into trouble. My discontentedness gets me entangled in sin. In my weaknesses I find myself "cast," flat on my back and unable to right myself. And I've made many self-sabotaging decisions out of fear and confusion. Psalm 23 is one of the best known passages in all of Scripture. But how often have we missed one of the most obvious points in this famous song? David sang, "The Lord is my shepherd." In other words, he sang "I am a sheep!"

Going Deeper Questions

1. How is a comparison with sheep an appropriate comparison for humanity? (Psalm 23:1-6, Psalm 100:3, Isaiah 53:6, Matthew 9:36)

   _____

   _____

   _____

   _____

2. Of the ways in which Jesus describes his goodness as a shepherd, which have you experienced? And which have you not experienced? (John 10:11-16)

   _____

   _____

   _____

   _____

3. How might you experience more of Jesus' goodness as a shepherd? (1 Peter 2:25)

   _____

   _____

   _____

   _____

Embracing Ordinary

Whatever you do, do it all for the glory of God.
1 Corinthians 10:31 (NIV)

G.K. Chesterton (1874-1936) was a journalist in London for more than 30 years. During that time, he wrote 4000 essays and authored 100 books. Arguably the most prolific writer of his time, he was truly extraordinary, with a unique personality, gifts and calling. For one, he was extraordinary looking. Standing 6'4" and weighing well over 300 pounds, Chesterton was larger than life. He often had a cigar in his mouth, a cape over his shoulders, a cane in his hand, and he wore tiny glasses that pinched his giant nose. He was a site to behold.

He was also extraordinarily absentminded. Usually lost or late for his next appointment, Chesterton could rarely remember where he was supposed to be or what he was supposed to be doing. He once famously telegrammed his wife writing, "At the market, where am I supposed to be?"

Finally, he was extraordinarily brilliant. For example, it's reported that he dictated his books and never rewrote a single word, not even having his secretary read back to him what he had dictated. A celebrated Christian apologist, Chesterton was famous for showing up late to debates, often with his clothing disheveled and his mind distracted. Sparring against the brightest thinkers of his day, he would easily win the hearts and minds of his listeners.

Chesterton's extraordinariness notwithstanding, one of my favorite quotes of his is about the value of being "ordinary." Chesterton wrote:

> The most extraordinary thing in the world is an ordinary man and an ordinary woman and their ordinary children.

We live in a world that pursues extraordinary at all costs. Adults drive themselves into the ground and parents pressure their children to be extraordinary. Yet, Chesterton claimed that the "most extraordinary thing" is embracing God's design in something as ordinary as the family and reveling in our role within it. Sadly, though, this type of most extraordinary life is often dismissed because it is so ordinary. It's not valued because it is so easily acquired. But that is the reality with all of God's greatest gifts. They are free.

What does all of this have to do with living for the glory of God? If

> *In the end, our call is not to be extraordinary. Our call is to be faithful, to bring God glory in all we do.*

we're not careful, our pursuit of an extraordinary life can lead to our missing out on life, even destroying it. Rather than reveling in the free gifts of God, however ordinary, we sell our souls in pursuit of the extraordinary. How many have pursued the extraordinary career, or bank account, or adventure only to shipwreck their lives and families? In the end our call is not to be extraordinary. Whole churches can be sucked into this temptation. Yet, our call is to be faithful, to bring God glory in all we do.

I'll give you a more personal example. I am not writing this book because I believe I am extraordinary, or because I want to become extraordinary. Although I have certainly battled that temptation. I know that I will never write like G.K. Chesterton. However, the older I get the more clearly I see the value of embracing the ordinary.

Embracing the ordinary makes life about God's glory, rather than about one's accomplishments and frees me to enjoy my gifts and calling, as well as my accomplishments. In the end, it is the freedom brought by embracing my ordinariness that allows me to write without fear. Embracing my ordinariness allows me to work diligently, taking even greater risks, knowing that I am living for God's glory rather than my own fame and/or fortune. No longer do I feel the burden to say something brilliant, to win an audience. Rather, I am free to offer my gifts, simply answering my calling and realizing that some people will connect with what I have to share and others will not. I write simply to add my voice to the choir, and I leave the rest up to God, praying that he is glorified in the effort.

Going Deeper Questions

1. What pressure do you feel to be extraordinary, and why do you feel that pressure?

_____

_____

_____

_____

_____

2. What does embracing ordinary mean to you and how will it bring greater freedom?

_____

_____

_____

_____

_____

3. What will letting go of extraordinary mean for you, and what steps will you need to take to do so?

_____

_____

_____

_____

_____

_____

4. How has God uniquely gifted and called you for his glory? Be sure to note both your strengths and your weaknesses.

_____

_____

_____

_____

_____

God's Presence

Where two or three gather in my name,
there am I with them. Matthew 18:20 (NIV)

I first heard this story when I was visiting a parishioner in the hospital, and I started crying immediately, right there in the hospital room. It probably will not provoke the same type of emotional response in others, but I will never forget this story.

The person I was visiting was chronically ill, and had been in and out of the hospital for the last five years. She had probably spent as much as a third of her life in the hospital over the last five years. Relatively young, in her mid-thirties, she has several different diseases. Her suffering is intense at times and we have prayed for years for her relief and healing, and we've seen God care for her in tangible ways over that time.

She possesses a strong faith in Jesus and is beloved by our congregation. Many folks within the church have joyfully helped to bear her burdens, and doing so has been a blessing for many. Although she has suffered greatly over the last few years, she has asked the Lord many times to use her illnesses as an opportunity to draw others close to himself and to bring himself glory. And, as often as she has been in the hospital over the last few years, she has had lots of opportunity to share with doctors and nurses her faith in Christ, and has invited many of her caregivers to church throughout the years.

Well, it finally happened. One of her caretakers actually started coming to church! I cannot describe how encouraging this has been for me, not to mention for this young woman who has suffered so much because of her illness. It has also been encouraging for the many others who have been caring for her over the last five years.

After years of sharing her faith in Jesus and receiving nothing but polite acknowledgement from doctors and nurses alike, one of the nurses has actually started attending the church. This means that God has heard and answered our prayers that this woman's suffering would be used as an opportunity to reach someone who may not have otherwise been a part of fellowship or heard the gospel.

This answer to prayer has been a great reminder to many that in God's economy none of our pain is every wasted. God is working all things together for the good of those who love him and are called according to his purposes (Romans 8:28). Even chronic illness and suffering can be used by God.

What was even more striking though was the nurse's description of her experience when she first walked into the church. This is the part that made me cry. Talking to my sick friend the nurse said,

> "When I walked into the church foyer that morning, I immediately felt what I had felt all those times in your hospital room, and I turned to my husband and said, 'This is where we are supposed to be.'"

I cried when I heard this story because it was a confirmation that the presence of God had been present all these years in the hospital and ministering to this nurse, while she cared for my sick friend. The nurse went on to describe to my sick friend how she had observed visitors to her hospital room pray and read Scripture, and of how she had often thought about the love being shown toward my sick friend.

Imagine, the presence of God so filling a hospital room that doctors and nurses who are in the room sense him there. Even if they don't know God themselves or recognize God's love being shown toward those who are sick, they still experience God presence in the midst of other believers, even believers who are suffering. How awesome is that! The Spirit of God is physically present, ministering in, among, and through his people, wherever two or more are gathered in his name, even in a hospital room.

Going Deeper Questions

1. What does Matthew 18:20 say about the importance of gathering with other Christians?

   _____

   _____

   _____

   _____

   _____

2. On a scale of 1 to 10, how committed are you to gathering regularly with God's people for worship, and what barriers exist to increasing the frequency of attendance in worship?

_____

_____

_____

_____

_____

_____

3. When and how have you sensed the presence of God among his people?

_____

_____

_____

_____

_____

4. How might you be more attentive to the presence of God when gathered with other believers in worship?

_____

_____

_____

_____

_____

Laughter

She can laugh at the days to come.
Proverbs 31:25 (NIV)

For the past 16 years, the conversation at our dinner table began with the same question, "Anything funny happen today?" I know it is not a particularly deep question. Even as I write the question out, it seems superficial. I am sure that there are lots of families with dinner table discussions that are weightier spiritually, as well as more biblically centered, but this question grew out of a desire, even a need, for laughter.

This will not come as a shock to anyone. Pastoral ministry can be difficult at times. People face lots of struggles in life and pastoral ministry is all about listening to and praying with and for folks who are struggling. Of course, it's a privilege to pray with and for folks, but it can also become a significant burden. In fact, there was a season in ministry when the burdens were so overwhelming that I began to experience physical symptoms related to stress. I am glad that season has passed. But, after a workday full of conversations on subjects like death, disease, divorce, and various sinful entanglements, I wanted to laugh. I needed to laugh.

In answer to the question, "Anything funny happen today?" we've heard some terrific stories, especially as my kids were teenagers. Stories like sneezing unexpectedly and blowing snot across the classroom, tripping in the hallway at school and spilling one's books all over the floor, and spending the whole day with one's zipper down, just to name a few. And we've laughed a lot around the dinner table, and the laughter was always helpful, and not just to me. It was helpful to my kids too. Laughter is good like a medicine (Proverbs 17:22).

Even more important than our need to laugh though is the recognition that laughter can reflect godly character. In the Old Testament book of Proverbs, we read that a person with noble character will "laugh at the days to come." It is true that some folks laugh more easily than others, which means that in some cases laughter is simply a part of one's personality.

> *A person with noble character can laugh at the days to come because their character is a reflection of their trust in the goodness of God.*

But laughing can also be a matter of godly character, which means that laughter can be cultivated in our lives. What link is there between having godly character and being able to laugh at the future?

A person with noble character can laugh at the days to come because their character reflects their trust in the goodness of God. People of noble character have built their lives on the belief that God will treat those who act upright with compassion and mercy. This means that no matter how difficult things become those with noble character can hope in God's goodness and fairness. They can do so because they have banked on these attributes in God's character during the good times.

For sure, there is a lot to be sad about in life, and a lot that requires a sober minded response, which means sometimes tears are the best response. But no matter how difficult life becomes, a person of noble character can laugh because they know who controls life.

Going Deeper Questions

1. Are you quick or slow to laugh, and why do you feel you are either quick or slow to laugh?

    _____

    _____

    _____

    _____

2. Are you able to laugh at the days to come, or are you afraid of the days to come? Give examples.

    _____

    _____

    _____

    _____

3. How might your quickness or slowness to laugh reflect your faith in God's goodness?

    _____

    _____

    _____

    _____

Dreams

"Your old men will dream dreams"
Acts 2:17 (NIV)

In the summer of 2004, I awoke in the middle of the night after having a dream that I knew was from the Lord. I prayed and asked God for the interpretation but did not immediately receive any insight. I slowly drifted off, back to sleep. The next morning, I went on with my day as usual.

A little over a week later, on a Sunday morning during our regularly scheduled pre-service prayer time, one of the folks who was praying with us relayed the contents of my dream to me. Make sure you understand. I had never told anyone about the dream. I had in fact forgotten about the dream.

Here's how it happened. That morning a small group of us were praying as we always do on Sunday mornings before the worship services, when my friend stopped in the middle of his prayer and said, "Kelly, while we were just now praying the Lord gave me a vision of…." He went on to detail exactly what was in my dream.

It would be easy for us to relegate God speaking through dreams to an ancient phenomenon. According to Scripture we know that God spoke through dreams to Daniel (Daniel 7:1), as well as Daniel's king, Nebuchadnezzar (Daniel 2:45). God also spoke through dreams to Joseph, Mary's fiancé. In one instance, telling him not to be afraid to take Mary as his wife (Matthew 1:20), and later directing him to flee to Egypt with baby

Jesus for safety (Matthew 2:13). Even more to the point though, the age in which we live is described in the book of Acts, as the age in which "your old men will dream dreams" (Acts 2:17).

While receiving dreams from God is not a daily occurrence in our age, neither is it unheard of. Clearly, the primary way in which God speaks to us is through the Bible, and the message God communicates to us in our dreams will never contradict Scripture. But, God also speaks, upon occasion, to some while they are asleep.

In case you are tempted to dismiss my dreams as unique to a pastor, I was at a fundraiser a couple of years ago when I heard the main speaker described to some 600 in attendance that he first began trusting in Jesus as Savior because of a dream that he had one night. Again, it would be easy to pass this off as emotionalism. But the speaker was a Yale educated, *New York Times* best-selling biographer, and a nationally syndicated radio host, who had first begun trusting in Jesus as Savior when he was an adult. His name is Eric Metaxas. While I would not recommend all he's written, I would recommend his book titled *Miracles*. It reads much like the book of Acts.

I used to think I was special because I received dreams from the Lord. I thought I was special until I read in the Old Testament book of Job that one of the reasons God speaks to us in our dreams is to turn us from wrongdoing (Job 33:14-18). In other words, God uses dreams is to reach those who are particularly dense and have not been reached through more conventional methods. Certainly, that was the case for Nebuchadnezzar and Joseph.

Now, I raise the reality of God speaking to us through dreams because it highlights God's deep desire to reveal himself to us, to make himself known. It is encouraging to know that God has made himself known to humanity through Jesus Christ, and that he continues to reveal himself.

Going Deeper Questions

1. What might have happened in Nebuchadnezzar's and Joseph's life if God had not spoken to them through dreams? (Daniel 2, Matthew 1:20)

_____

_____

_____

_____

_____

2. How does it encourage your faith to think of God speaking to us through our dreams?

_____

_____

_____

_____

3. How does it challenge your faith to think of God speaking to us through our dreams?

_____

_____

_____

_____

Receiving from God

Whatever you ask in prayer, believe that you
have received it, and it will be yours.
Mark 11:24 (ESV)

About ten years ago, I attended a funeral for a teenage boy who had died in a car accident. I was not officiating the funeral but arrived a little early nonetheless and found the family seated at the front of the auditorium comforting one another. It seemed like it was going to be a uniquely difficult service. Funerals for young people are always difficult, and the grief was heavy in the room. I slipped into a seat near the back.

Over the next fifteen minutes the church started to fill, but the pastor had not yet arrived, which made me feel a little nervous. The family was visibly grieving up front and it seemed that they could use some guidance. A couple minutes before the service was scheduled to start, the father of the deceased teenager stepped to the microphone. He was obviously shaken by the loss of his son, understandably so, and he began to address the congregation. The pastor was still nowhere to be seen.

Through tears he explained how much he loved his son, that his life had been tragically cut short, and that he had brought a bottle of oil, with which he was going to anoint his son's dead body. It was at that point he invited us to bow our heads and join with him in prayer, asking in Jesus' name and believing that the Lord would raise his son from the dead.

When he bowed his head to pray, I slipped out of the auditorium and went looking for the pastor. He was in his office preparing his remarks for the service. By the time we returned to the auditorium, the father had already anointed his son's body. The pastor made his way down to the casket, where the father was standing over his son, praying. The pastor gently slipped his arm around the father and stood beside him for a minute. When the boy did not return to life, the pastor helped the father to his seat and began the service.

The point of my sharing this story is not that the father was foolish. Frankly, I would not put it past myself to do something similar. Grief can drive us to take desperate steps, and I do believe that God can raise the dead. In fact, I believe that God has raised the dead. In fact, he has raised his Son form the dead, Jesus Christ. My question is what are we to make of the promise of God in Mark 11:24? The father had asked in prayer, believing that he would receive his son back from the dead. Why didn't we see a miracle?

> *Faith is essential and faith is powerful, but our believing that we have received what we ask for cannot determine the future.*

And do not get me wrong. I have seen miracles. I have seen people physically healed, hard hearts softened and reversals of fortune through prayer. In fact, not a day passes that I do not join with someone in prayer asking for a miracle. But what are we to do when we ask in prayer believing, and nothing seems to happen? What are we to then think of the promise in Mark 11:24?

The short answer is that we are to understand that our faith cannot force God to do we want. Faith is essential and faith is powerful, but our believing that we have received what we ask for cannot determine the future. Only God determines the future.

The point is that we are told by Jesus to believe that whatever we ask for in prayer we will receive. In other words, prayer is powerful, and faith is important. However, we are not told to believe that we will receive through prayer whatever we want. The trick of praying in faith and receiving what you have asked for is to first hear from the Lord what/how he would have us to pray, so that we can pray in accordance with his will.

Going Deeper Questions

1. When have you experienced a "mountain moving" answer to your prayers?

   _____
   _____
   _____
   _____
   _____
   _____
   _____

2. When have you asked but not received a "mountain moving" answer to your prayers?

_____

_____

_____

_____

_____

_____

_____

3. Hearing from the Lord about what/how we are to pray can be difficult. Describe your habits of listening for the Lord's voice?

_____

_____

_____

_____

_____

_____

_____

4. How much faith is needed to experience miracles, and how would you describe your faith at this time? (Matthew 17:20)

_____

_____

_____

_____

_____

_____

_____

Excuses vs. Reasons

Whose weakness was turned to strength.
Hebrews 11:34 (NIV)

I recently ran in an adventure race called the *Tough Mudder* with three other guys. Adventure races require the endurance needed to run longer distances combined with the strength needed to overcome large obstacles. It took my group four hours to cover 11 miles and clear 22 obstacles, as we traveled at the lightning-fast pace of just under three miles per hour. Not too impressive.

I was the oldest in our group by 14 years and clearly the weakest link. At one point in the race, I was complaining about something that hurt when I looked up and there in front of me was a man wearing a t-shirt on the back of which was printed this quote, "Excuses are the nails that build a house of failure." Embarrassed by my excuse making and wanting to justify my whining, I began to wax eloquent about the differences between making an excuse and offering a reason. Distinguishing between the two can be difficult I explained to my captive audience. I'm sure that they listened only because they had nowhere else to run, literally.

An "excuse" is an explanation offered to justify our actions, while a "reason" is an explanation offered to help others better understand our behavior. This means that when it comes to matters of faith, an excuse is offered to avoid consequences and/or continue in sin. A reason, however, is offered to better understand the causes that led to one's sinful behavior, which is always a necessary precursor to escaping from sinful entanglement.

Here's the good news. Whatever the reasons for our sinful behavior, through faith in Jesus we need not be trapped by our past. Through faith in Jesus our weaknesses, whatever they may be, are turned to strength and there is no need to spend our lives making excuses. Take Rahab for example. I'm sure that there were good reasons for her poor decision to live as a prostitute (Joshua 2-6). It's not hard to understand why people enter that line of work. But through faith in God, she escaped the condemnation that her entire city received. Rahab's story challenges those who use their woundedness as an excuse to avoid taking steps of faith.

Gideon's story also challenges us to live by faith and to stop making excuses. Gideon was the leader who famously "fleeced" God. Gideon's army was originally 32,000 strong, but by faith he willingly trimmed it to only 300 soldiers (Judges 6). Gideon's story challenges those who use their doubts and/or fears as an excuse to avoid taking steps of faith. Samson's story also challenges our excuse making. Samson thoughtlessly betrayed himself and his people out of lust. In the end, it was only after his eyes were gouged out that he could finally see the truth (Judges 13-16). Samson's story challenges those who are using addiction as an excuse to avoid taking steps of faith.

Here's the point. Excuses are always readily available. But so are reasons. There are always good reasons why our favorite sins are our favorite sins; my parent's divorce, my father's absence when I was a child, my sense of dislocation as we moved all over the country when I was a teenager. This is just a small list of the reasons I have sinful weaknesses in my life, and Rahab, Gideon and Samson each had reasons for why they wrestled to trust God. But through faith in Jesus our weaknesses are turned to strength. The invitation of the gospel is to live by faith in Jesus, who empowers us to escape the reasons we turn to sin and to say no to the excuses that we are tempted to embrace.

Going Deeper Questions

1. How has excuse making kept you from taking steps of faith in times past?

   _____

   _____

   _____

   _____

2. How might understanding the reasons for sinful behavior better enable you to take steps of faith?

   _____

   _____

   _____

   _____

3. What faith steps is God calling you to take?

   _____

   _____

   _____

   _____

Excellence and Idolatry

Well done, good and faithful servant!
Matthew 25:23 (NIV)

I have shared in fellowship with Christians all over the globe: Colombia, China, Cuba, Rwanda, and Mexico, to name a few. If you have ever shared in worship with Christians outside of America, then you have probably noticed that the American church has tremendous resources. I'll never forget singing during a worship service in Rwanda unaccompanied by any instruments. At first, I thought Rwandan's were simply opposed to using instrumentation in worship. I later learned that the congregation could not afford instruments.

In Cuba I attended a worship service in what was little more than a garage. Only ten folks were present in the worship service that morning. The floor was made of dirt where we stood singing, except where they had laid down boards so that we did not have to stand in the mud. The guitar player had only four of the five strings needed for his instrument. In both settings though, Rwanda and Cuba, the joy in worship was real and the presence of the Lord was powerful.

Yet, the battle cry in the American church over the last couple of decades has been for "excellence" in worship. Pastors have called for excellence in worship, both vocally and instrumentally, as well as for excellence in things like social media and video production. Every element of the service is highly choreographed and produced for excellence.

The explanation that is most often provided for placing so much emphasis on excellence is a mix of pragmatism and theology. Pastors explain that Americans are expecting excellence, and anything less would result in a missed opportunity for the gospel. Some even say that anything less than excellence would be a barrier to worship.

The term "excellence" is as a term of comparison though, with some church programs or worship experiences being described as excellent, while others being evaluated as subpar. This leads me to ask, "What if I am not excellent in my gifting and my service is below par?" What if when compared to others, I fall far short of excellence?

> *A job worth doing,*
> *is worth doing well.*
> *We certainly should not*
> *waste our gifts and*
> *opportunities by giving little*
> *effort in God's service.*
> *It is also true that a*
> *job worth doing, is worth*
> *doing poorly.*

Should I be prohibited from serving, from utilizing my gifts? If, as an American, I'm not excellent, then should I move to Cuba or Rwanda to serve? It's true that I have not heard anyone in the American church suggest that Cuban or Rwandan church programs should match the quality of excellence we have in America, but that still misses the point. We are tempted to worship excellence, rather than God.

It is true that a job worth doing, is worth doing well. We certainly should not waste our gifts and opportunities by giving little effort in God's service. It is also true that a job worth doing, is worth doing poorly. In other words, the Lord is worthy of our service, even if I cannot do it excellently, because faithfulness in serving the Lord is always the best thing, regardless of the quality of the service.

In the end, as I evaluate the call to excellence within the American Church, it often seems to be little more than a call to idolatry, as we make the utilization of our gifts and our time serving about us, rather than about God's glory. Biblically, the call upon our lives is never excellence, it's always faithfulness. Furthermore, the goal in service is never to be excellent. The biblical goal in our service is always God's glory, which rightly places the emphasis of our service and the focus of our energies on faithfulness.

Going Deeper Questions

1. How is the goal of faithfulness different than the pursuit of excellence?

_____

_____

_____

_____

_____

_____

_____

2. How does the goal of faithfulness both encourage and challenge you in your service?

_____

_____

_____

_____

_____

_____

_____

3. Where/how have you seen the American church emphasize excellence over faithfulness?

_____

_____

_____

_____

_____

_____

4. What risks in service have you failed to take, because you did not feel as though you would be able to serve with excellence?

_____

_____

_____

_____

_____

_____

Representative Leadership

Shepherd the flock of God that is among you, exercising oversight, not under compulsion, but willingly, as God would have you; not for shameful gain, but eagerly.
1 Peter 5:2 (ESV)

During the first few years of my service as senior pastor, selecting church leadership was bumpy at times. In some cases, there was politicking and even campaigning for positions on the elder board. I often heard things like, "The eight men on the board should represent each of the various demographics within the congregation." It surprised many to learn though that biblically, elder leadership is not designed by God to function like the United States Congress.

Many congregants falsely believe that when electing elders, they are selecting someone to represent their opinions and preferences, believing that those for whom they voted are charged to secure what they want or to at least push in that direction. This is not the case. The church is not to be run as a representative democracy, with constituents vying for influence through leadership or lobbying for a particular agenda. This may be why Paul "appointed" elders in each of the churches that he started, to avoid this type of confusion (Acts 14:23, Titus 1:5).

While elders are certainly called to care for the needs of those they shepherd, which includes being aware of and sympathetic to their desires, the function of elders is not to represent the opinions or preferences of the people to God. The purpose of elder leadership is to represent the thoughts and actions and priorities of God to his people. Elder leadership is certainly a type of representative leadership, but only in that elders serve as God's ambassadors to his people.

This means that campaigning and/or politicking for leadership positions within the church is out of place. We are called to pray for our church leaders, not try and manipulate and/or control them. Elders can be affirmed by a congregation through a voting process. There is certainly nothing wrong with voting for a slate of elder nominees, but nominees should be put forward for vote only after being vetted by other elders and being found to have a lifestyle of godliness that matches the New Testament qualifications (1 Timothy 3:1-7, Titus 1:5-9).

This also means that once elected to serve as an elder, keeping the people of the church happy is not an elder's responsibility. The responsibility of elders is to support and encourage faithfulness within the lives of the people they shepherd. Elders are to call the people to increased dependence upon Jesus, which will include leading them into and through difficult circumstances at times, as well as calling them to carry their cross.

For those who serve as elders this is a tremendous responsibility that requires humility. The responsibility of elder leadership is complicated by the reality that elders are both shepherds of God's flock, as well as sheep within the flock of God. As shepherds, it is of the utmost importance for elders to remember that they are also sheep. Elders are both following the Good Shepherd, as well as responsible for helping others follow him.

Going Deeper Questions

1. What type of governance does your church use?

   _____

   _____

   _____

   _____

2. Would you say that your church operates as a representative government, or do the elders act as ambassadors, representing God to the people?

   _____

   _____

   _____

   _____

3. What is our attitude to be toward our Elders (1 Timothy 5:17, Hebrews13:17)?

   _____

   _____

   _____

   _____

4. How can you be praying for your Elders?

   _____

   _____

   _____

   _____

Persevering to Produce

The seed on good soil stands for those with a noble and good heart,
who hear the word, retain it, and by persevering produce a crop.
Luke 8:15 (NIV)

In August 1914, Ernest Shackleton and a crew of 27 men set sail from London. Their goal was to cross the continent of Antarctica, but their ship soon became trapped in ice. Frozen in place, the crew drifted with the ice field for ten months. They were finally forced to abandon their ship as the ice began to crush the ship's hull, pushing much of the ship under the water.

Forced off the ship they camped on the ice, waiting for an opportunity to use their lifeboats to row for safety. After another six months of waiting, they decided they must try for land regardless of the danger. After floating for seven days in the South Atlantic, they finally spotted a small island, named Elephant Island. Safely camped on Elephant Island, Shackleton left his crew behind and went for help.

Over the next 17 days, Shackleton crossed the world's most treacherous seas, covering 800 miles in a 22-foot lifeboat. He finally landed at a whaling station on South Georgia Island. However, when he attempted to go back to pick up the rest of his crew, he was unable to rescue them because of ice blockage. Over the course of the next four months, he tried two more times to rescue his crew and failed. He was finally able in August 1916 to make the rescue, a full two years to the month after setting out from London.

Much to his surprise, he found the crew waiting with their bags packed. When asked how they knew that he was arriving that day, they told him that they didn't know when he would arrive. They went on to explain that every morning they packed their gear in preparation for his arrival. At night, when no rescue was made, they would unpack their gear, only to repack again in the morning. In this way they daily unpacked and repacked for four straight months.

As Christians, we are in a similar position, left behind, wondering when Jesus will return to rescue us from our trials and struggles. We wait for the day when Jesus will return and take us to a place of safety, a place of perfect peace, without tears, trials, and hardship.

To persevere spiritually requires habits that increase our strength while we wait upon Jesus to return.

It wasn't enough that Shackleton's crew waited on the shores of Elephant Island each day for rescue. To persevere, they woke each morning and packed their bags. This discipline of daily packing and unpacking was a discipline needed to persevere in that harsh environment. The realities of the world in which we live are too difficult spiritually to simply exist as God's people. To endure while we wait, we will also need daily disciplines to persevere. To persevere spiritually requires habits that increase our strength while we wait upon Jesus to return.

I'm fond of telling my kids, "we get better at what we do every day." What can we do every day, so that we persevere in our faith? I would imagine that the activity of packing every morning and unpacking every night probably felt mundane and futile to the sailors in Shackleton's crew. But it was this little discipline that helped them to persevere until rescued.

We often want a silver bullet spiritually speaking. We want that one shot, that one activity, that miraculously puts us over the top and solves all our problems. I just do not see that in Scripture. Instead, I see a call to perseverance in activities that may feel mundane at times, but activities through which God works powerfully. Packing and unpacking felt mundane, but help Shackleton's crew to maintain the focus and hope in a harsh environment.

Going Deeper Questions

1. How would you describe your current sense of hope that Jesus will return to rescue his people from their troubles? Why?

_____

_____

_____

_____

_____

_____

2. What daily activities of persevering do you practice? (Luke 9:23)

_____

_____

_____

_____

_____

_____

_____

3. What benefits have you experienced through the daily practice of these disciplines?

_____

_____

_____

_____

_____

_____

_____

4. What practice/s might you begin to strengthen your spiritual productivity?

_____

_____

_____

_____

_____

_____

_____

Growing Grass

Man shall not live on bread alone, but on
every word that comes from the mouth of God.
Matthew 4:4 (NIV)

It's funny the passing comments one remembers. A long-time parishioner met me in the foyer one Sunday morning, after I had just finished preaching, and he said to me, "Good feeding pastor." That was probably eighteen years ago now. I'll never forget it though.

Although his words were encouraging to me, as I certainly want to do a good job in the pulpit each week, the Holy Spirit also used them to remind me that it is only God's Word that "feeds" us. We live on every word that comes from the mouth of God, not on the words that come from a preacher.

As a pastor, a shepherd of God's people, I am reminded daily that shepherds do not grow grass. Only God can grow grass. Instead, shepherds simply lead their sheep to the grass. That's what shepherds are to do, lead and guide sheep to green pastures, to places of nourishment. Similarly, it's always tempting to think that my words feed the congregation each Sunday. But only God's Word feeds us. Only God can nourish his people. Instead, my job as a pastor is to lead the sheep to the grass, to point the sheep toward the place where they can find nourishment.

This means that anytime we are caring for others spiritually, whether we are parents caring for our children, or a Sunday school teacher caring for those in our class, or a counselor caring for clients, our job is to point those for whom we are caring to the Scripture. Our job is not to try to create food (i.e. grow grass), but rather to simply direct them to the nourishment that God has already made available for us in his Word. Ultimately, it is only the truth of God's Word that satisfies, sustains, and strengthens God's people.

It is tempting to offer our own words of wisdom when guiding others spiritually, or the popular psychology of the day, but the greatest need we have is to hear the truth of God's Word. Don't misunderstand me. Psychology has its place. After all, all truth is God's truth, wherever it may be found. Yet, our greatest spiritual needs are always met through Scripture, as the Holy Spirit ministers the truths of God's Word to our hearts. It is the Scripture that is "useful," because it is the Scripture that is "God-breathed" (2 Timothy 3:16).

When Jesus was led into the wilderness to be tempted by Satan, he fasted for forty days. Can you imagine going without food for that long? When Satan finally came to tempt him, Jesus must have been very hungry and felt very weak. But that's not at all how Jesus is portrayed during the temptation. Instead, Jesus appears to have crystalline clarity during the experience and answers each of Satan's temptations with God's Word. The conclusion we are left to draw is that although Jesus had gone without physical sustenance for 40 days, he had been feasting on God's Word and was stronger because of it. Man lives on every word that proceeds from the mouth of God.

Going Deeper Questions

1. How often do you read Scripture during the week and what passages of Scripture do you most often read/avoid?

   _____

   _____

   _____

   _____

   _____

2. How have you experienced God's Word feeding and nourishing your soul?

   _____

   _____

   _____

   _____

   _____

3. When and how might you feed on God's Word more regularly? What barriers must be overcome to feed on God's Word more often.

   _____

   _____

   _____

   _____

   _____

Healing and Time

I am the LORD, who heals you.
Exodus 15:26 (NIV)

After the divorce, her ex-husband had quickly remarried and moved the kids to the other side of the country. For two decades she had no contact with her children. Zero! Not a phone call, not a letter, nothing.

As time passed though, something powerful happened, something miraculous. It wasn't fast, but it was thorough. Through a relationship with Jesus, the pain of her sinful decisions, the loss of her children and the divide in the family was slowly healed.

First, Jesus touched her shame and guilt and pride, covering her with the medicine of forgiveness. Instead of running from God, she learned to run to him, confessing her sinfulness and waiting upon his care. She began counseling to process her loss. She gathered with prayer partners to seek God's healing. She found a place of service in her local church.

Thousands of miles away, her children were also being cared for by Jesus. Of course, she had been praying for them daily, hourly at times, but there had been no contact for 20 years. Then an email came. Where dozens of letters had gone unreturned, her children were now reaching out to her with words of forgiveness—words about how they had known God's care and about how they wanted to know their mother. While healing is still ongoing in this family, the mother and children are being reconciled to one another.

Rose Kennedy, the matriarch of the Kennedy family, said this about healing.

> It has been said, 'Time heals all wounds.' I do not agree. The wounds remain. In time, the mind, protecting its sanity, covers the wound with scar tissue and the pain lessens. But it is never gone.

Of course, Mrs. Kennedy suffered tremendous loss in life. She had nine children, one of whom died during WWII in a plane crash and two others who were assassinated while serving in public office. I would agree with Mrs. Kennedy though. Time is the space in which healing happens, but the passing of time alone doesn't bring us healing. Believing that time alone heals wounds, is like saying that "Garages fix cars." Garages are the spaces in which cars are fixed. But garages don't fix cars. Someone in the garage fixes the cars. Mechanics fix cars. The same is true with healing. Someone must work within the space of time to bring healing. That someone is Jesus.

Although time doesn't heal all wounds, the good news of the gospel is that Jesus heals all wounds in time. Left unattended we may feel less and less of the pain caused by abuse, or a divorce, or a death, but without the touch of Jesus, our wounds remain, even fester, just below the surface. Without the touch of Jesus, we learn how to cope with the pain as a scar forms. Time doesn't heal all wounds, but time is the space in which Jesus is working to heal all wounds.

In the Old Testament book of Exodus, God reveals himself as our healer. The context of the passage is the Israelites' first stop in the wilderness, after miraculously crossing the Red Sea. They had no water, but God miraculously provides them with water to drink, and tells them "I am the LORD, who heals you" (Exodus 15:26).

Of course, the promise of healing for Israel is available to all people through Jesus. We begin the process of receiving God's

> *Time doesn't heal all wounds, but time is the space in which Jesus is working to heal all wounds.*

healing as our faith in Jesus cancels the debt of sin that separates us from God (1 Peter 2:24). Jesus also offers us healing emotionally, repairing the wounds that we have inflicted upon ourselves and suffered from others, as well as mentally, setting our thoughts in order and renewing our minds. Admittedly, the healing may come slowly, and there is no promise of complete healing this side of heaven. But the good news of the gospel is that God either provides healing in this life, or the grace sufficient to endure the brokenness present in this life. For example, the Apostle Paul struggled with what appears to have been a physical malady and received the assurance of grace sufficient to endure it. Paul wrote:

> Three times I pleaded with the Lord to take it away from me. But he said to me, "My grace is sufficient for you, for my power is made perfect in weakness." 2 Corinthians 12:8-9 (NIV)

Remember this is the same guy whom the Lord used to heal others, simply through the touch of his handkerchiefs (Acts 19:12). God's grace is sufficient for all our healing through faith in Jesus Christ.

Going Deeper Questions

1. What wounds have you suffered in life, and how have you experienced God's healing thus far?

   _____

   _____

   _____

   _____

   _____

2. What healing would you like God to provide for you in the days ahead?

   _____

   _____

   _____

   _____

   _____

3. How has God provided you with grace sufficient to endure as you wait upon healing?

   _____

   _____

   _____

   _____

   _____

Church Discipline

Hand this man over to Satan for the destruction of the flesh, so that his spirit may be saved on the day of the Lord.
1 Corinthians 5:4-5 (NIV)

We need to deepen our understanding of church discipline. The truth is that church discipline is a lot like an iceberg, with much of it happening below the surface and going unrecognized as biblical discipline. In many cases, we experience discipline and never even know it. For example, discipline takes place every time we read Scripture (Hebrews 4:12), and any time we hear the Scripture preached publicly (2 Timothy 4:2), and every time we pray together (Matthew 6:9). Any time Scripture is read aloud or declared or discussed the Spirit is at work shaping and transforming us into the image of Christ.

Obviously, some church discipline is to be done above the surface of the water, publicly and more demonstrably (1 Corinthians 5:4-5, 1 Timothy 5:20). Yet, even the most severe discipline, that of handing someone "over to Satan," is to be done with the hope that their "spirit may be saved on the day of the Lord." In other words, the aim of *all* biblical discipline is ultimately the repentance and salvation of the one being disciplined. For this reason, church discipline is primarily designed to restore God's children when they fall into sin (Matthew 18:15-20). Rather than being merely punitive, we are to lovingly confront and correct each other so that we may all enjoy salvation (Hebrews 10:24).

Strategically, church discipline is to happen first in private (Matthew 18:15). If the offending party remains unrepentant, the offended person should meet again privately with the offender, taking along two or three witnesses. This is designed to establish the validity of the offense and provide a stronger call to repentance (Matthew 18:16).

If, after a second attempt at discipline, the offending party remains unrepentant, the offended person should bring the matter to "the church" (Matthew 18:17). At a practical level, this usually includes a meeting with a pastor or the Elders in charge of caregiving. If all attempts at calling someone to repentance and reconciliation have failed, the offender is to be treated as a non-Christian, and removed from fellowship (1 Corinthians 5:13). This is what Paul means by handing them "over to Satan." This step of being publicly removed from fellowship (i.e., handed over to Satan) is most often the step pictured in our mind when we think of church discipline. The truth is though that this step is to be the last step in a long disciplinary process. Bear in mind that to treat someone as a non-Christian, by handing them "over to Satan," does not mean that those in leadership believe they know whether the person being

> *As shepherds of the flock of God we must understand that God is presenting his Son a "bride," not brides.*

disciplined is, or is not, a Christian. Only God knows who is being saved. To discipline someone in this manner is to simply treat them as a non-Christian, because their lack of repentance is consistent with that of a non-Christian.

As an aside, additional care is to be exercised in disciplining church leaders. First, we are not to entertain charges against leaders without the testimony of at least two or three witnesses (1 Timothy 5:19). This is important because leaders are uniquely vulnerable to slander. If a leader sins in a manner that violates their office (1 Timothy 3), we are to rebuke the leader publicly as an example to the congregation (1 Timothy 5:20).

In secular organizations, leaders often feel pressed to choose between the lesser of two evils when disciplining employees, weighing the good of the whole against the good of the individual. But in the Church, the good of individuals and the good of the community are never at odds. Because we are all "one body," what is good for an individual person within the Church is good for all the people within the church, and what is good for all within the church is good for each individual (Romans 12:5). Remember, God is presenting his Son a "bride," not brides (Revelation 19:7), which means as individuals we are a part of a larger integrated whole. Although the church is made up of many individuals, we are one community and must act accordingly. Ultimately, the belief in unity among the Body of Christ, his people, and the importance of maintaining that unity is preserved through church discipline, not threatened.

Going Deeper Questions

1. By whom are you currently being disciplined in the church?

    _____

    _____

    _____

    _____

2. How do you feel your church currently views discipline?

    _____

    _____

    _____

    _____

3. When have seen public discipline done well within the church?

    _____

    _____

    _____

    _____

    _____

4. When have seen public discipline done poorly within the church?

    _____

    _____

    _____

    _____

    _____

Sin's Inequality

All have sinned and fall short of the glory of God.
Romans 3:23 (NIV)

I visited someone in jail yesterday. It's always humbling to visit folks in jail, as I'm reminded of just how little separates me from them. While I have not committed the sin for which this person is being held, I am a sinner just as he is, which means I am in need of God's grace and mercy every bit as much.

Whenever I visit someone in jail, I always remind them of God's offer to forgive anyone who will confess their sin and repent (1 John 1:9). The death of Jesus was sufficient to cover every possible sin, and forgiveness is offered to us through faith in Jesus, no matter how heinous our behavior. As I was sharing the gospel yesterday with this man, he must have sensed my desire to offer him some reassurance of God's love because he remarked, "Oh well, all sin is equal in the eyes of God."

"That's not true," I said. I went on to explain that it's true that all have sinned and that all sinners are equally valued by God. But, I said, "It is not true that all sins are equal. Some sin is worse than other sin. After all, if all sins were equal that would mean murdering someone is no worse than punching them. How could that be possibly be the case?" The American judicial system recognizes the difference between punching someone and murdering them. How much more would the God of the universe distinguish between lesser and greater sins?

The truth is that there is a hierarchy of sin. That's why God gave the Ten Commandments, which clearly outline the most important sins to avoid, those sins with the gravest consequences upon our relationship with God and one another. In fact, we can safely infer that all the other sins, the ones that number eleven through infinity, aren't as bad as the top ten, which God took the time to write on stone and gave to Moses (Exodus 31:8).

Even within the Old Testament law, sins varied in how they were treated, with the nature of a sin committed being matched with a punishment of appropriate severity. For example, while someone was to be put to death for taking another person's life, they were certainly not to be put to death for coveting someone else's possessions.

Here's the point. If we pretend that all sins are equal, then we run the risk of diminishing the holiness of God and the power of the gospel. The truth is that the death of Jesus is sufficient to cover all sins, both big and small. Moreover, all sinners, both the most heinous sinner who ever lived and the most righteous person who ever lived, need to receive the grace of God offered through Jesus' death. You see, although all sins are not equal, all sins are equally separated from our Creator. No matter whether it's gossip or murder, all sins equally separate us from God, who is holy and dwells in unapproachable light (1 Timothy 6:16). This means that no matter how trivial or heinous our sin might be, we are all in need of forgiveness. That's why it is humbling to visit prisoners in jail. There we are reminded of our need for God's mercy every bit as much as those who have committed the most heinous of crimes.

Going Deeper Questions

1. In what ways is it relieving to learn that not all sins are equal?

   _____
   _____
   _____
   _____
   _____
   _____

2. In what ways is it a challenge to learn that not all sins are equal?

   _____
   _____
   _____
   _____
   _____
   _____

3. How is the gospel even more beautiful in realizing that not all sins are equal?

   _____
   _____
   _____
   _____
   _____
   _____

Personality and Character

*I praise you because I am fearfully
and wonderfully made. Psalm 139:14 (NIV)*

Mom dragged me and my siblings to church every Sunday morning, as well as most Sunday evenings and Wednesday nights. It seemed that anytime the doors were opened, we were at the church, and I'm thankful for that spiritual heritage at this stage in my life. Growing up in the church there were certain phrases heard constantly, but which no one ever bothered to explain. Like the phrase, "God is shaping us into the image of Jesus."

It was only as an adult that I realized what this phrase does and does not mean. This phrase doesn't mean that God is changing my personality. It means that God is changing my character, making me more like Jesus in my behavior. Few people ever think about the difference between their personality and their character. But to change our personality would mean to change the unique design given to me by God—the fearful and wonderful parts that make me, me (Psalm 139:14). Personality includes things like how we express ourselves to others (i.e., whether we are loud or quiet), and how we make decisions (i.e., whether we are information limiting or embracing), and what energizes us (i.e., whether we like crowds of people or alone time). One's personality is morally neutral, neither right nor wrong. Our character on the other hand is our moral makeup, whether we make God-honoring decisions and/or selfish and self-destructive decisions.

The philosopher Soren Kierkegaard said, "Now with God's help, I will become fully me." What does this mean? It means that if you're an extraverted, task oriented, kinesthetic learner before trusting in Jesus as Savior, which I was, then that won't change after receiving him into your life. God wouldn't want it to change those things about me in fact, because God isn't looking to change our personalities. He's looking to change our character.

Now, it's true that our personality impacts our character, and vice versa. For that reason, it can take a lot of work to discern the difference between the two in any given situation. Extroversion and introversion are a matter of personality and God is great with our staying just the way he made us. However, God does not want us to stay an arrogant extrovert or an arrogant introvert. Here's where the shaping takes place. God is in fact molding us into the character of Jesus. Arrogant folks refuse to do what they are told. They won't submit, whether it's arrogant kids that won't submit to their parents, or arrogant employees that won't submit to their boss. We know we are humble when we are obedient and submitted to God's Word.

It's tempting to label some as arrogant if they are loud, or energetic or opinionated, or passionate, or competitive or ambitious, but none of these personality traits necessarily preclude humility. Remember, the meek inherit the earth, not because they are weak, but because they are obedient to God. In other words, meek and weak are not synonymous. Someone can have a dominant personality and still be humble, just as someone can have a very quiet personality and still be arrogant. Much of the hard work of maturing spiritually involves enjoying our personality while asking God to change our character.

Going Deeper Questions

1. What type of personality do you have?

   _____
   _____
   _____
   _____

2. How do you see God changing your character?

   _____
   _____
   _____
   _____

3. How does your personality impact your character, and how does your character impact your personality?

   _____
   _____
   _____
   _____

4. How do you see God blessing your personality?

   _____
   _____
   _____
   _____

Two Brothers

At that time the son born according to the flesh
persecuted the son born by the power of the Spirit.
It is the same now. Galatians 4:29 (NIV)

Once upon a time there were two brothers. They were half-brothers to be exact, having the same father, who was named Abraham, but two different mothers. The name of the older brother was Ishmael, and his mother was named Hagar. It's not a pretty part of Abraham's family tree. In fact, it's hard to wrap our modern minds around, but Hagar was Abraham's slave.

Abraham was married to Sarah, but Sarah had been unable to have any children, and this despite the fact that God had promised them children. In an act of desperation, Sarah and Abraham decided it would be best for Abraham to sleep with Hagar, who was Sarah's servant, in order to bear the son that they so deeply desired, the son God had promised them. Although not God's will for them, this solution was legal in their culture. In this way, the child would be born to Hagar, but would be considered Abraham's and Sarah's son by law.

When Ishmael was born to Hagar there was a lot of celebrating. Everyone was happy. Until the strangest thing happened. Sarah became pregnant. Thirteen years after Ishmael's birth to Hagar, Isaac was born to Sarah, and Abraham became a father once again. Hagar and Ishmael immediately felt like second class citizens, and Ishmael began to persecute Isaac. The tension in the home was so bad that Abraham was forced to make a decision between his son of the Law (Ishmael), and his Son of Promise (Isaac). In the end, Abraham sent Ishmael and Hagar away, solidifying Isaac's place as the heir within the family (Genesis 21:1-21).

The Apostle Paul used the story of these two brothers to raise a spiritual question in the book of Galatians. The questions is: "Are we going to rely upon our own abilities to secure the favor of God, or are we going to rely upon God's abilities to provide us with the favor he has promised us?" Ishmael was a product of Abraham, Hagar and Sarah relying upon their own abilities to secure God's blessing. Isaac, on the other hand, was a product of God's abilities, providing Abraham and Sarah with the son that he had promised to them. Upon whom do we rely, ourselves or God?

> *Today, those who have put their confidence in the flesh, their own abilities, still laugh at and ridicule those depending upon God's promises for salvation.*

Paul maintains that we will either rely upon our own performance of the law, our own efforts to keep the commandments of God in an effort to earn God's favor, or we will rely upon God's performance—God's wisdom, knowledge, timing and grace—to provide us with all that he has promised to us through faith in Jesus. And make no mistake, there will be lots of pressure to doubt God's promise of salvation through faith in Jesus. In fact, that's why Paul wrote the book of Galatians. Christians were being pressed in Galatia to rely upon themselves for salvation, rather than continuing to rely upon God. The son born "according to the flesh," Ishmael, persecuted the son "born by the power of the Spirit," Isaac, and we can expect the same. You can imagine. Can't you? It's easy to picture Ishmael as a teenager, laughing at the little boy Isaac, teasing and taunting him in an attempt to undermine his confidence in God's promises that he would be the rightful heir.

Today, those who have put their confidence in the flesh, their own abilities, still laugh at and ridicule those depending upon God's promises for salvation. What does this look like? It looks like those who are religious pressuring those who are relying solely upon God's promise to embrace the notion of conditional acceptance. Most of the time the pressure is subtle and sophisticated, with those who are religious appealing to guilt and shame to motivate acts of faith. The subtle inference is that to be accepted by God we need to do more religious activities, things like: read our Bible more, attend worship services more often, give more money to the church, or serve more. Of course, all these activities are good, and are activities encouraged in Scripture. But they are not the basis of our hope for salvation.

The gospel is that we are saved by God's grace apart from anything we do (Ephesians 2:8-9). That means we are saved not by our performance, that is by our works, but rather by depending upon the performance of Jesus, his works. God graciously and miraculously applies the good works of Jesus to our account, as we trust in his death for the forgiveness of our sin and his resurrection for life eternal. God did for us through Jesus, what we could not do for ourselves, just as God gave Sarah a son (Isaac) that she could not provide for herself. All the other religions in the world encourage people to trust in their own behavior for salvation. Only Christianity calls us to trust in the behavior of another person for salvation—Jesus Christ.

Going Deeper Questions

1. How does the story of Ishmael's and Isaac's birth reflect the beauty of the gospel?

   _____

   _____

   _____

   _____

2. When have you ever been laughed at or mocked for believing the gospel?

   _____

   _____

   _____

   _____

3. When have you felt pressure to depend upon yourself for salvation?

   _____

   _____

   _____

   _____

Yoke of Slavery

It is for freedom that Christ has set us free.
Stand firm, then, and do not let yourselves be burdened again
by a yoke of slavery. Galatians 5:1 (NIV)

A yoke is what a cow or ox wears around their neck to pull a load. Picture in your mind's eye wooden bars, one lying across the animal's shoulders and the other across the animal's chest, with leather straps connecting them to one another and tying them to a wagon or plow. A yoke is an instrument of labor, under which an animal toils. The "yoke of slavery" to which Paul refers is the Old Testament Law. Although not meant by God to be a burden, the Law became a burden, under which the people toiled and by which they were enslaved because of their sinfulness. Even though they wanted to keep the Law, they were unable to bear the load. It was simply too heavy.

How did the Law become a burden? The Law became a "yoke of slavery" because it revealed the sin present in humanity. God's law revealed that humanity cannot love God or one another as required (Matthew 22:36-40). The yoke imagery is helpful, because our enslavement to sin is not dissimilar to the weaknesses of animals being revealed through their toil. Cows are massive creatures, with tremendous strength and endurance. It's hard to imagine them growing tired under the burden of a yoke, but after only a couple of hours of plowing or pulling a wagon, their weaknesses are revealed.

Humans, although powerful both intellectually and physically, similarly had their sinful weaknesses revealed as the yoke of the Law was laid upon us. The good news though is that the Law was given for this very reason, to show our sinfulness and our utter need for God's grace. For this reason, God gave the Law as a "tutor," teaching us of our need for his grace, or a "guardian," caring for us until God's grace in Christ was revealed (Galatians 3:24).

How were the Galatians to avoid being burdened "again" by the "yoke of slavery"? The answer was by avoiding circumcision. In Galatia, Christians were being pressured to trust in Jesus *plus* keep the Old Testament Law to be assured of their salvation. And the ancient symbol of one's commitment to keep the Law was circumcision. Yet, Paul declared:

> For in Christ Jesus neither circumcision nor uncircumcision has any value. The only thing that counts is faith expressing itself through love. Galatians 5:6 (NIV)

By "counts," Paul means "saves." Faith in Jesus is the only thing that counts because it's the only thing that saves! Circumcision does not "count," because it cannot save. In fact, we cannot be saved by doing anything. Paul's point is that we shouldn't burden ourselves with making a commitment to keep the Law, because it won't result in salvation. In fact, the law only ever resulted in our enslavement to sin being revealed. That's why he described it as a "yoke of slavery."

The good news is that Jesus kept the Law perfectly, and as we trust solely in Jesus's law-keeping we can be assured of our salvation because it will produce a love for God and others within our lives, an outcome which trying to keep the Law was never able to produce.

Going Deeper Questions

1. How is the message of faith in Jesus is all that "counts" a message of freedom?

   _____

   _____

   _____

   _____

2. If we are free *from* the Law and the "yoke of slavery," what are we free *to* do, be, or become? (Galatians 5:14)

   _____

   _____

   _____

   _____

3. How is the yoke of the Law different from the yoke of Jesus? (Matthew 11:28-29)

   _____

   _____

   _____

   _____

   _____

Training vs. Trying

Train yourself to be godly.
1 Timothy 4:7 (NIV)

Do you know the difference between "trying" and "training?" Trying is to make a singular attempt. For example, to try is to walk up to a barbell, which holds a weight that you've never attempted to lift before and give it all the strength you must get it off the ground. Training, on the other hand, is the work of gradually building strength over time by regularly practicing an activity. If I want to lift a heavy barbell and had never lifted that much weight before, then training would include going to the gym three or four times a week, beginning with much smaller weights and building strength over time through repetition, so that I would be able to eventually lift the full weight.

Too many Christians are simply trying to follow Jesus, rather than training for godliness as followers of Jesus. Don't get me wrong. It's great that we try to follow Jesus! I'm sure that God would much rather that folks try to follow Jesus, than to not try at all. But simply trying to follow Jesus rarely results in godliness. In fact, simply trying to follow Jesus often results in the spiritual equivalent of a pulled muscle—what is often referred to as spiritual burnout. Some of us have tried to pray for hours without stopping, or tried to fast for a week straight, or tried to give 10% of our income to the church, or tried to memorize an entire book of the Bible, and all without ever having built up any strength in these habits.

It's heroic to try, but often trying results in tragedy, which then leads to discouragement. Let's be honest, how many of us have either said to ourselves, or heard someone else say, "I tried that once, but it didn't work for me." There is a better way. Instead, of simply trying to follow Jesus, we are to train ourselves in godliness as followers of Jesus. How will Christians go from drowning in contemporary culture to living lives of godliness? The answer is by slowly building spiritual strength over time through disciplined repetition of an activity. In fact, discipline is essential to a life discipleship.

Jesus even trained (Mark 1:35, Luke 5:16). He moved from faithfulness in the little things to the greatest act of faithfulness in the history of the world—obediently giving his life on the cross as a sacrifice. So often we visualize only the spectacular moments in Jesus' ministry, but there were many, many other moments of quiet, humble, diligent discipline in which Jesus trained.

If you are someone who seldom prays, then begin with praying only for a few minutes a day. Don't jump into the deep end of the pool. That's where people drown. Start in the shallow end and build strength. The question is not so much, "What is my prayer life like today?", but rather, "What do I want my prayer life to be like in a year?" We should ask ourselves, what do I want my Scripture knowledge to be like in a year? What do I want my giving habits to be like in a year? What do I want my evangelism temperature to be like in a year?

God is calling us to train ourselves in godliness. Stop simply trying to follow Jesus and let's begin training ourselves in godliness as followers of Jesus.

Going Deeper Questions

1. How are you currently training in godliness?

   _____

   _____

   _____

   _____

   _____

2. What have been some of the benefits of training for your life?

   _____

   _____

   _____

   _____

   _____

3. Where in your life do you need to do some training, but continue to simply try?

   _____

   _____

   _____

   _____

4. What training activities might you begin to gain strength?

   _____

   _____

   _____

   _____

Moon Jumping

Do not use your freedom to indulge the flesh;
rather, serve one another humbly in love.
Galatians 5:13 (NIV)

There are generally three responses to the message of God's grace. Some believe it's too good to be true. These folks can't believe that we're saved apart from anything we do, solely by trusting in Jesus, and they often respond by trying to keep God's law. These are called "legalists," so called because of their effort to merit God's favor by keeping his Law. To the extent that we hope our good behavior will earn God's favor, we are legalists. In fact, you may be a legalist if you're thinking, "Doesn't God want us to try to be good?!" Yes, God is pleased when we try to be good, but he is not willing to pretend that we are anywhere close to perfect in our character.

The effort required for moral perfection, which is the requirement for salvation, could be compared to the physical effort needed to jump from the earth to the moon. While God is certainly pleased that we try to clear the moral distance between him and us, he is not going to pretend that we come anywhere close to actually making the jump successfully. In God's righteousness, he will not overlook the fact that we are unable to match his perfect moral character. What God did do though, was come to the earth himself, live a sinless life, effectively clearing the behavioral equivalent of the distance between the earth and the moon. Then he died as a sacrifice for our sins, absorbing the punishment that we deserve (John 3:16).

A second response to God's grace through faith in Jesus is that of "license." License is the posture of giving ourselves permission to do whatever we want. We can double our efforts to show God how righteous we are, making an effort to harness the flesh, which is legalism. Or we can lapse into license, which is to indulge the flesh in all types of sinful activities. Biblically, our "flesh" is our natural disposition toward sin, with which we are all born.

To use the moon jumping analogy, those who take license with God's grace don't resent the fact that they can't jump to the moon, morally speaking, as the legalists do. Rather, those who respond to the message of God's grace with license, don't even try to jump at all. Instead, they abuse the freedom they have been granted from the consequences of sin by indulging in even more sin. License is fueled by the belief that we can live like Hell, because Heaven is our future home. Ever make a sinful decision because you knew God's grace is sufficient to cover the sin? That's license. That's indulging the flesh.

There's a third way of responding to the message of God's grace. It's the way of "liberty," and it's the God honoring response. Realizing that God's grace, through faith in Jesus, frees us from our sin, a response of liberty is a lifestyle focused on enjoying God's favor. Rather than attempting to harness the flesh, and trying to demonstrate one's righteousness, and rather than indulging the flesh, in a posture of abusing God's grace, those who respond with liberty use their newfound forgiveness to crucify the flesh (Galatians 5:24). To use the moon jumping analogy, responding with liberty is to see the distance that Christ jumped for us and work to emulate his character, conduct and concerns in every area of one's life. The goal in a life focused on liberty is not to try to merit God's favor, but to honor God with one's life.

Going Deeper Questions

1. How do you try to merit God's favor, and how might the call of God to freedom give you greater peace?

   _____

   _____

   _____

   _____

2. What sins are you indulging, and how might seeing God's grace in Christ give you greater freedom?

   _____

   _____

   _____

   _____

   _____

3. Whom might you better serve in humble love because of your freedom in Christ?

   _____

   _____

   _____

   _____

   _____

Inside Out Change

Do not leave Jerusalem, but wait for the gift my Father promised, which you have heard me speak about. For John baptized with water, but in a few days you will be baptized with the Holy Spirit.
Acts 1:4-5 (NIV)

I struggled with panic attacks as a teenager. Gripped by fear, I would break into a sweat and begin trembling uncontrollably. It was as if all the adrenaline in my body was released at once, and I would shake and convulse. These episodes would last for ten or fifteen minutes, and I would rock back and forth and wring my hands through my hair, while tremors moved through my body. I remember praying for peace and strength, and thinking, "I bet the first disciples didn't struggle with things like this!" I realize now they struggled too.

Too often, we marvel at God's work *through* the first disciples, all the while forgetting about God's work *in* those same men's lives. We cannot have it both ways. Either we believe that God worked powerfully in *and* through the first disciples, or we believe that the first disciples were powerful in and of themselves.

Peter walked on water and was the first to preach the gospel publicly, with three thousand converted in one day. He served as pastor of the church in Jerusalem and wrote two of the New Testament's books, not to mention being martyred for his faith. But Peter was also the disciple who denied the Lord three times, and not before pulling a sword in the Garden of Gethsemane and cutting off the ear of one of the high priest's servants. Jesus even implied that Satan was working through Peter at one point. Peter was a loudmouthed, hotheaded, aggressive man who was only able to do great things for God because he was transformed by God's power.

John also did amazing things. Often referred to as the "beloved," John was the only disciple brave enough to attend Christ's crucifixion. Consequently, he was the only one Jesus addressed from the cross, the one whom Jesus asked to care for Mary, his mother. Persecuted for his faith, John was later banished to the island jail of Patmos, a desolate island off the coast of Turkey. Yet, nowhere in his writings is there any complaining. Instead, it's on Patmos that he pens the final book in the New Testament, the book of Revelation.

> *The truth is that discipline, no matter how effective, never reaches the root of our need for inner change.*

We cannot forget though that it was also John, along with his brother James, who were together nicknamed the "Sons of Thunder." Several stories in the Gospels give us glimpses of why this nickname fit them so well, like the time they encouraged Jesus to call fire from heaven to consume a city because of its residents' refusal to receive Jesus' message. And the time they asked Jesus to guarantee them the two most prominent positions of authority in his kingdom. James and John were self-centered and power-hungry men who consistently placed personal interests above the good of the group. Yet, they were transformed by God's power.

From a human perspective, James, John, and Peter did not provide a promising start for the church. Without the transforming power of God at work in their lives, I would not want them on my basketball team, and certainly not my church leadership team. But the Holy Spirit brings real and lasting change in our lives, and he is still at work today. In fact, Jesus distinguishes between his baptism with the Holy Spirit and John the Baptist's baptism with water, because it highlights the significance of the Holy Spirit's ministry. John the Baptist's baptism was a public commitment to trying harder. If a Jew had forsaken the Law, then a posture of repentance—that is confession of sin and a commitment to embrace the Law—was expected, and water baptism was the symbol of one's repentance. The problem was that John's baptism didn't provide any power. The repentant person walked away from John's baptism unchanged.

Jesus' baptism with the Holy Spirit is categorically different because we are changed on the inside, rather than simply soaked on the outside. Through the baptism of the Holy Spirit, we receive God's power within us. While John the Baptist's baptism simply encouraged greater discipline in keeping the Law, the gift of the Holy Spirit delivers the resurrection power of God directly to us (1 Corinthians 6:19).

The truth is that discipline, no matter how effective, never reaches the root of our need for inner change. We can white-knuckle our way to sobriety or fidelity, but the desire for alcohol or the longing to flirt with someone other than our spouse will remain. Only through the presence of the Holy Spirit, can we be changed from the inside out. As the Holy Spirit changes our hearts, the desire we have for sin begins to wane and our longings for godliness begins to increase.

For a long time, I tried to overcome my panic attacks by sheer force of reason, telling myself over and over that there was nothing to be afraid of. "There is nothing to fear but fear itself," I'd chant in desperation. My attempts to manage the attacks helped some, just as twelve-step groups play a role in helping overcome addiction. But white-knuckling through my panic attacks fell far short of providing internal confidence. Only the Holy Spirit provided real confidence and peace, as he ministered the truth of God's goodness to my soul, a truth that came through memorizing Scripture.

Going Deeper Questions

1. How are the examples of change in the lives of men like Peter and John, both encouraging and challenging?

    _____

    _____

    _____

    _____

    _____

    _____

    _____

    _____

    _____

    _____

2. How have you experienced God at work in your life to bring change?

_____

_____

_____

_____

_____

_____

_____

_____

_____

_____

_____

3. In what areas of your life/character do you still need the Holy Spirit to bring change?

_____

_____

_____

_____

_____

_____

_____

_____

_____

_____

_____

The Power Needed

Apart from me you can do nothing.
John 15:5 (NIV)

It was my first-time meeting with this couple. The husband explained that after a decade of marriage, neither of them thought they would be able to continue. Both were recovering drug addicts. They had met in drug rehab. Not a strong indicator that they would be able to make the marriage work. Both were also previously divorced, and both were survivors of childhood sexual abuse. To date, they had also both done years of extensive individual and marital counseling. The husband explained that I was their last-ditch effort to save their marriage.

Feeling completely overwhelmed by their issues, I sat quietly for a moment, trying to absorb the weight of all that had been disclosed. What could I offer these folks that they had not already heard or tried? How could I possibly help them? After a long and awkward silence, I sheepishly confessed, "I'm not sure what to say." "What?" the husband blurted. "I don't have any wisdom to offer you guys," I said. I remember their blank stares. It occurred to me that the family who had referred them to me, probably oversold my counseling abilities.

"But," I quickly added, "I can pray with you, if you'd like." At that the husband's eyes rolled wildly, he guffawed, and rather contemptuously asked, "Pray together?" "Yes," I said, "prayer gives God an opportunity to do what we are unable to do ourselves." "Okay," he said, glancing at his watch.

We had been together less than 20 minutes at that point, and I was sure that he regretted coming. We bowed our heads together and I prayed. The prayer lasted about 15 seconds and there were no lightning bolts. I simply asked God to heal their marriage. The earth did not shake and I am sure they wondered how quickly they could get out of my office. I said, "Amen," shared with them a short Scripture, and I let them know that I would be happy to pray with them again anytime. We said an awkward goodbye and I figured that I would never see them again.

About three months passed. I am sure that my surprise at hearing his voice was obvious even over the phone. It was the husband who called. He said, "Pastor, would you mind doing that prayer therapy with us again?" "Sure," I said quickly, and then I asked him how things had been going in his marriage. "Well," he said, "I have been shocked at how my wife and I are more patient with one another, and the only thing I can figure is that maybe the prayer therapy worked." He said the words "prayer therapy" as if it were some new technique for healing. We set another date to get together.

When they arrived, the husband shared that he had only ever attended church on holidays, and never really felt any need for religion. "But," he added, "it really seemed to help us to pray, so I'm willing to give it a try." It was clear that he had never prayed to receive salvation, so over the course of the next couple of minutes I shared with him the gospel and asked if he would like to first pray to receive the forgiveness of his sin. He said yes quickly, which caused his wife to burst into tears. She was bawling so hard that I stopped to ask her if everything was okay.

"It's just that I've been praying for some time that he would be saved," she said. I led the husband in prayer to receive Christ as Savior, as well as prayed for their marriage, asking God to continue to change the way they related to one another and to strengthen their commitment to one another. After I prayed, they prayed together, for one another, for the first time.

Too often we are tempted to rely solely upon our own wisdom, and if this couple had come with lesser issues I might never have admitted my inadequacy. I am sure I would have prayed with them and shared Scripture, but I am afraid I would not have depended primarily upon the Holy Spirit's intervention. Clearly, unless the Holy Spirit did something for this couple they would never have been changed, and it is exactly this type of power that is needed in life.

For the longest time, I thought that following Jesus was primarily about discipline—the discipline needed to read my Bible and obey what it taught. I thought the power needed for life was within myself. Do not get me wrong. Discipline is important to a life of discipleship, but I have grown to see that following Jesus is primarily about dependence upon the Holy Spirit, because apart from him we can do nothing.

For this reason, when I want to see changed in my life, I am learning not to throw more discipline at the needed change. Instead, I am learning to invite the Holy Spirit to change my thoughts and desires (Romans 12:2, James 1:14), and to strengthen my faith. As the Holy Spirit works in my life, I find that I no longer desire sin and I am increasingly able to honor him with my life. The good news of the gospel is that the same power that raised Jesus Christ from the dead is available today through the Holy Spirit—power to overcome sinful habits and to experience real and lasting change. It is only through the Holy Spirit's movement and work in and through us that we bear any fruit at all.

Going Deeper Questions

1. What activities in your life are directly aimed at increasing your dependence upon the Holy Spirit?

    _____

    _____

    _____

    _____

    _____

2. How have you seen God work in and through you, providing the power needed for life?

    _____

    _____

    _____

    _____

    _____

3. What steps can you take in your life to increase your dependence upon the Holy Spirit?

    _____

    _____

    _____

    _____

The Insanity of Sin

Do not be deceived: God cannot be mocked.
A man reaps what he sows. Galatians 6:7 (NIV)

The 1977 hit song titled *Only the Good Die Young* was written and sung by Billy Joel. At the time, the song was highly controversial, because the lyrics traced the thoughts of a young man in his efforts to pressure a young woman into having sex with him, outside of marriage. The Catholic Church attempted to have the song banned from radio stations, but those actions only seemed to fuel record setting sales. Here is verse four.

> They say there's a heaven
> for those who will wait
> Some say it's better
> but I say it ain't
> I'd rather laugh with the sinners
> then cry with the saints
> The sinners are much more fun...
> You know that only the good die young.

Is goodness punished and sin rewarded? Although Billy Joel and the Apostle Paul didn't agree on the value of doing good, they would have certainly agreed on the difficulty of doing good. Doing good isn't always easy, and we can become weary in the effort. Nonetheless, Billy Joel's theology notwithstanding, Paul insisted that goodness is rewarded by God, and that we should persevere in doing good, even when it's difficult.

Goodness for Paul is "moral excellence," not a subjective reality. Biblically, "goodness" is an objective reality, existing outside of us, and defined by the character of one who never changes. In other words, we don't get to decide what is good. As popular as "alternative facts" may be in our day, goodness is defined by God's person, and our role is to simply acknowledge what is good and live accordingly.

Jesus made this very point when someone greeted him saying, "Good teacher, what must I do to inherit eternal life." Jesus responded with, "Why do you call me good? No one is good but God." Jesus was pressing the man to acknowledge that he was more than simply a good teacher. He was God in the flesh (Mark 10:18, Luke 18:19), the revelation of goodness in the world, and Paul went so far as to tie a failure to be good to a posture of mocking God. If we're skeptical about whether goodness is really the best strategy in life, believing things like "only the good die young," then it is God we are questioning.

This is what makes sin an act of insanity. To commit sin is to think and act like a crazy person, someone out of their mind, because it is to think and act contrary to the very person whose character defines goodness and controls the universe. Sin is irrational, contrary to everything that makes sense, because it is contrary to the character of the Creator, the one only one who is truly good and sustains our life. In other words, when we lie, cheat, steal, or act selfish in any way, it always leads to our destruction because it is contrary to the character of the one who gives us life.

Of course, the good news of the gospel is that although we are not good, and although we are all daily tempted to embrace Billy Joel's theology, God himself came to earth, lived a sinless life, and then gave his goodness as a substitute for our badness, dying on the cross to pay the penalty for our sins. As if that were not enough, God's Spirit dwells with all those who are trusting in Jesus for salvation, and it is by the Spirit that we can now pursue goodness.

Going Deeper Questions

1. Where do you see sin (i.e. insanity) in your life, and how has it led to destruction?

   _____

   _____

   _____

   _____

2. Where do you see goodness (i.e. sanity) in your life, and how has it led to life?

   _____

   _____

   _____

   _____

3. How can you experience life? (Galatians 6:7-10)

   _____

   _____

   _____

   _____

Zombie and Vampire Christianity

I know your deeds; you have a reputation of being alive, but you are dead. Wake up! Revelation 3:1-2 (NIV)

The Church in Sardis had a reputation for being spiritually "alive," but it was dead. How does this happen? One of the first things you notice in the passage describing this church is that there is no mention of persecution, which makes their experience unique among the seven cities listed in the book of Revelation. Scholars describe Sardis as a uniquely wealthy city in Asia Minor, whose inhabitants enjoyed peaceful lives free of difficulty. In Sardis the Christians were not suffering at the hands of either the Jewish or the Roman authorities, which stands in stark contrast to the experience of Christians everywhere else in Asia Minor.

In Ephesus the believers had persevered and not tolerated wicked people in their midst. In Smyrna, the Christians faced persecution from the synagogue of Satan. In Pergamum they had been lured into idolatry by false teachers. In Thyatira they had tolerated false teachers and were called to actively separate from that Jezebel. But in Sardis, there appears to have been neither internal strife nor external pressures. It seems that the church in Sardis had carved out for itself a peaceful coexistence with the secular culture, and in that climate many who were active in the church had never actually trusted in Jesus as Savior. They had "deeds" that looked as though they were spiritually alive, but they had not been born again. They were spiritually dead.

Churches all over America face the possibility of confusing spiritual activities with spiritual life. Many people are busy in American churches, much like in the church of Sardis. And many churches in America have a good reputation. Yet, the people within those churches may be dead, having never trusted in Jesus as Savior.

Does the Church in America face challenges? Sure! But compared to our brothers and sisters around the globe, the church in America lives in peaceful co-existence with the secular culture, not unlike the church in Sardis. For this reason, many American church-goers have a reputation for being alive, but are in fact dead and need to wake up.

Being physically active but spiritually dead might be best described as "Zombie" Christianity. Think about it. The Church of Sardis was active, having lots of good deeds and a reputation for being alive. However, like zombies, they only

> *While Zombie Christianity has lots of activity without any real spiritual life, Vampire Christianity is for the most part action-less, although possessing an insatiable interest in the blood of Jesus.*

appeared to be living. While the Church in Sardis most likely had some people who were alive spiritually, apparently many within the church were only a shell of activity. Not unlike a Zombie, many were only going through the motions, and they lacked any real life.

Of course, Zombie Christianity is not to be confused with "Vampire" Christianity. While Zombie Christianity has lots of activity without any real spiritual life, Vampire Christianity is for the most part action-less, although possessing an insatiable interest in the blood of Jesus. Vampire Christians want the blood of Christ, which provides for the forgiveness of our sins, but not the body of Christ, which is a lifestyle of identifying with the sufferings of Christ. Vampire Christians want God's grace without living a life that honors God through disciplined living.

The fix for Vampire Christianity is cross carrying, while the fix for Zombie Christianity is to "wake up." Zombie Christians must repent from their empty deeds and turn to a full dependence upon Jesus for salvation (Revelation 3:3). Repentance is marked by confession of sin and a turning away from sin toward dependence upon Jesus. Make no mistake, there will still be good deeds and a reputation of being alive after the Zombie Christians repent, but those activities will now flow out of a real spiritual awakening.

Going Deeper Questions

1. What is the danger of "Zombie" and "Vampire" Christianity to the broader church?

_____

_____

_____

_____

_____

_____

_____

_____

_____

_____

_____

2. What is the danger of "Zombie" and/or "Vampire" Christianity to an individual?

_____

_____

_____

_____

_____

_____

_____

3. How does the American culture contribute and/or encourage both "Zombie" and "Vampire" Christianity?

_____

_____

_____

_____

_____

_____

_____

Real Power

You will receive power when the Holy Spirit comes on you; and you will be my witnesses in Jerusalem, and in all Judea and Samaria, and to the ends of the earth. Acts 1:8 (NIV)

I've wrecked several cars. One time, I hit a barn with a friend's car. My excuse was that I didn't see it in my rearview mirror. I hit the barn so hard that I split open my forehead, as it bounced off the head rest and then into the steering wheel. I've also wrecked numerous motorcycles. In fact, I decided to sell my most recent motorcycle when my children were young, because I kept doing stupid things on it. I'll never forget wrecking my motorcycle over by the Wheaton College track.

I had parked it on the sidewalk outside the track. After running a few laps (a very few) I felt pretty masculine, so I decided to gun the throttle as I left the track. My goal was to jump off the curb and land in the street. I gunned it and the next thing I knew I was lying in the grass on the far side of the street. My motorcycle cleared the curb easily enough, but when it landed in the middle of the street, I lurched backwards rolling the throttle backwards again, which launched me a second time. Narrowly missing a tree on the other side of the road, I laid the motorcycle down softly in the grass. I was never more thankful for a helmet, although not because it protected my head from injury, but because it protected my face from recognition. I felt so embarrassed as the drivers of oncoming cars slowed to stare at me while they were passing.

Unfortunately, the more power something has the greater the probability I will wreck it at some point. But we all like power. Don't we? And Jesus promised us power. The primary purpose for God's gift of the Holy Spirit is so that we have the power needed to live as witnesses of Jesus. Through the Holy Spirit we now have the power necessary to communicate the good news effectively. And by communicate effectively, I don't simply mean the words we speak, but the lives we lead. After all, we all know that people are watching how we live as much as, if not more than, listening to what we say. It was the transformed lives of the earliest disciples that were the most convincing proof of the gospel. Men who were previously full of doubt and self-preservation, were powerfully changed to men of faith and self-sacrifice.

When the Holy Spirit descended upon the believers in Jerusalem they were changed, and the result was that the message of the gospel began immediately going out. The Church was formed, and they began living as bold witnesses for Jesus causing:

- Mass conversions (Acts 2:41)
- Devotion in prayer (Acts 2:42)
- Miracles, signs and wonders (Acts 4:31, 5:12)
- Moral excellence (Acts 5:1-11)
- Conviction in preaching (Acts 7:1-53)
- Generosity with financial resources (Acts 4:32)
- Compassion toward the weak (Acts 6:1)
- Perseverance in suffering (Acts 7:54-8:1)

We tend to believe that the first believers were instantly made mature when they received the gift of the Holy Spirit. But that's not the case. The earliest believers had to mature in their faith every bit as much as we must mature. On the day of Pentecost, when the Spirit came, Peter stood up and preached to thousands. Never mind that just a few weeks earlier he had denied Christ three times. It was also Peter who after receiving the Holy Spirit, alienated new Gentile believers by refusing to eat with them for fear that his Jewish friends would criticize him (Galatians 2:11-14). It took the Apostle Paul's rebuke of his behavior before he humbly acknowledged his wrong and stopped his hypocrisy.

John Mark quit halfway through a mission trip. When the going got tough, he went home! (Acts 13:13) It was Barnabas who came alongside John Mark and encouraged him and strengthened his faith. But do you remember Paul's response to John Mark's weakness? Was he patient and compassionate? No! He was harsh and dismissive. Paul rejected John Mark, refusing to include him on the next mission trip because he felt he was soft and couldn't be counted on (Acts 15:36-40). Later however, Paul grew in patience. In fact, so impressed by the fruit of Barnabas' work with John Mark that he requested that John Mark be included again in the mission effort (2 Timothy 4:11, Colossians 4:10).

Illusion always leads to disillusionment. Don't live with the illusion that the earliest believers didn't need to mature because you will be disillusioned by your own need to mature. I was so proud of myself last winter. I road my first snowmobile and didn't wreck it. There are few motor vehicles as powerful as a snowmobile and I was proud that I restraint and didn't wrap it around a tree. I'm maturing. Being completely honest with you though, it took everything in me not to launch that snowmobile off the side of the mountain. Several times I fought back the urge to see if I could set a new land-speed record. I can spend my days discouraged, focusing on the number of vehicles I've wrecked, or I can spend my days focusing on learning how to handle the power I have been given. The same is true spiritually. We can spend our days discouraged over missed opportunities to live as Jesus' witnesses or we can focus on being filled in the days ahead.

Going Deeper Questions

1. How are the stories of maturing in Peter's, Paul's and John Mark's lives encouraging, as well as challenging?

   _____

   _____

   _____

   _____

2. How have you matured in your witness for Christ?

   _____

   _____

   _____

   _____

   _____

   _____

   _____

3. How would you like to mature in the days ahead?

   _____

   _____

   _____

   _____

   _____

   _____

   _____

4. What practical steps can you take toward maturing?

   _____

   _____

   _____

   _____

   _____

   _____

Biblical Math

*That all of them may be one, Father, just as you are in me
and I am in you. John 17:21 (NIV)*

For the last couple of years, I've taught a class
titled *Introduction to Ethics* at the local community college.
On day one of class, lesson one is all about "worldview."
We each possess a particular perspective on life, by which
we judge what is right and what is wrong, and having
students work to understand their worldview is the first
step in recognizing whether their perspective is accurate.

Of course, as Christians the question is not simply
"What's our worldview?" but does our worldview match
God's. Clearly, God's perspective on life is the most
accurate perspective. In fact, much of the discipline
involved in discipleship, is the work of renewing our mind
(Romans 12:2), allowing God to change our perspective
so that we increasingly see the world from his vantage
point. Take, for example, relationships.

On the night before his crucifixion, Jesus prayed
that all Christians would be one (John 17:21). Of course,
the "oneness" for which Jesus prayed is not simply the
result of believing the same things, or of physically caring
for one another. Our beliefs and our behavior are certainly
a part of being "one," but unity goes far beyond mental
and physical "oneness." The unity that Jesus asked for
among his followers is a spiritual reality that transcends
this world and has always existed within the Trinity. Read
closely. Jesus prayed that we would be one "just as" God
the Father and God the Son are one.

Later, he reiterates this request, asking "that they may be one as we are one" (John 17:22). Is that our worldview? Do we see our unity with one another "just as" the unity shared between God the Father and God the Son? Do we see our relationships with other Christians as a supernatural experience that transcends this world and is tied to the unity within the Trinity?

The Bible teaches that God is one, but having three distinct persons, Father, Son and Holy Spirit. We most often teach our children that 1 + 1 + 1 = 3, but that's not biblical math, at least not when it comes to the nature of God. When talking about God, 1 + 1 + 1 = 1. Trinity means "tri-unity," which means that within the Trinity there is both intimacy and individuality.

Do we see our relationships with other Christians as a supernatural experience that transcends this world and is tied to the unity within the Trinity?

Each person within the Trinity is fully God and each shares completely in all parts of divinity, but each person is also a unique individual (Matthew 28:19-20). The good news of the gospel is that for all those trusting in Jesus for salvation, we are made one "just as" God is One. Through faith in Jesus, the second member of the Trinity, we are brought into relationship with every member of the Trinity, as well as into relationship with all people of faith.

Why does this matter? It matters because everything we'll ever need is found "in" relationship with Christ. All the intimacy and individuality (i.e., personal fulfillment) that we so desperately long for is found as we experience the Trinitarian community. In Christ, we are made a new creation (2 Corinthians 5:17). In Christ, we become "partakers of the divine nature" (2 Peter 1:4), empowered by the Holy Spirit's presence in our lives.

Through the Holy Spirit's presence "we are more than conquerors" (Romans 8:37) enabled to do all things to which God has called us (Philippians 4:13). In Christ, we receive all that we need for life and godliness (2 Peter 1:3). In Christ we are loved and forgiven (John 3:16). In Christ we are adopted into God's family and redeemed from our sinfulness (Ephesians 1:5-7). In Christ we are raised "to walk in newness of life" (Romans 6:4). In Christ we are no longer slaves to sin (Romans 6:5-6), but we are made alive with him (Ephesians 2:5).

Remember the phrase "just as"? Just as God the Father, God the Son and God the Holy Spirit experience intimacy and identity within the Trinity, we experience intimacy and individuality through our unity with God through faith in Jesus.

Going Deeper Questions

1. What about a "biblical" worldview is easy/hard for you to understand or embrace? How is your world view uniquely biblical? In what respects is your world view not biblical?

_____

_____

_____

_____

_____

2. How have you experienced increased intimacy and individuality through faith in Christ?

_____

_____

_____

_____

3. How might growing in an understanding of being "in" Christ address old wounds in your life, as well as strengthen your sense of self?

_____

_____

_____

_____

_____

Divine Care & Human Responsibility

You have too many men. I cannot deliver Midian into their hands,
or Israel would boast against me, 'My own strength has saved me.'
Judges 7:2 (NIV)

God called Gideon to deliver Israel from the
Midianite army. But as Gideon was getting ready to go out
to battle, God did something strange. He directed Gideon
to reduce the number of soldiers under his command by
over 99%. Most generals want as much manpower as they
can gather, but God directed Gideon to say to the soldiers
in his army, "Anyone who is afraid, can go home." With
that invitation, 22,000 Israelites went home, leaving only
10,000 soldiers at Gideon's side. And God wasn't
finished. He said to Gideon, "There are still too many
men," and he told him to take the remaining men to a
nearby watering hole, where he would further "thin them
out." There, at the water's edge, Gideon was to, "Separate
those who lap the water with their tongues, as a dog laps,
from those who kneel down to drink" (Judges 7:5). A
strange evaluation process to be sure, but of the 10,000,
only 300 lapped the water as dogs, and God told Gideon
that he was to use only those 300 in battle.

God reduced Gideon's soldiers to less than 1% of
his original fighting force. If we lost 99% of our resources
today, would we still believe that God is able to provide?
Of course, Gideon's 300 defeated thousands of Midianite
soldiers, and to make the feat even more amazing all that
they used in the battle were trumpets (Judges 7:22). It was
miraculous.

Now, the confusing part for many in following Jesus is understanding the relationship between divine care and human responsibility. In other words, since it's God who gives us the victory, how do we know what *we* are to be doing? What is our responsibility?

To answer this question, let's first make sure to note that God did use 300 men to defeat the Midianites. In other words, while God could have just as easily destroyed Midian's army without any help, he chose to involve 300 men. Make no mistake. Dependence upon God is not a passive posture of inactivity. Dependence upon God is an active posture of engagement through obedience. Gideon and his 300 men were actively engaged in the victory God provided to them, and God continues today to use his people to build his Kingdom.

This means that we are actively involved in the victories that God is providing for us through obedience to his commands. For example, everything in Scripture indicates that we are to participate in our salvation, which is the greatest victory that God is providing for us. Don't misunderstand me. We don't cause or secure our salvation. God saves us, we don't save ourselves, but we do actively participate in our salvation. Just as a baby doesn't cause their birth, although actively participating in the birthing process, we are born again by God's power and called to participate in the gift of spiritual new life (John 1:13). Whatever battle we may be facing today, dependence upon God for the victory requires an active posture of engagement through obedience to God's commands.

The challenge with obedience though is that it often feels strange to us. Imagine how strange Gideon must have felt about sending away over 99% of his fighting force. In fact, looking at the list below, how often do we hesitate to embrace these types of activities because they feel strange.

- Singing to one another (Colossians 3:16)
- Confessing to one another (James 5:16).
- Praying for one another's healing (James 5:17).
- Fasting secretly for God's reward (Matthew 6:18)
- Loving our enemies (Matthew 5:44).
- Giving sacrificially (2 Corinthians 8:7).
- Boasting in the Lord (1 Corinthians 1:31).
- Forgiving others (Colossians 3:13).
- Avoiding sexual immortality (Ephesians 5:3).

If we are depending upon ourselves, these activities will seem at best strange, and at worst foolish. But, if we are depending upon God, these activities of obedience will be glorious opportunities to experience God's power and victory.

Going Deeper Questions

1. What about Gideon's story is challenging and/or encouraging to you personally?

   _____

   _____

_____

_____

_____

_____

_____

_____

_____

_____

2. What are some activities of obedience that feel strange to you?

_____

_____

_____

_____

3. How have you seen God work through your obedience to provide and protect you?

_____

_____

_____

_____

_____

4. What activities of obedience might you begin to embrace more thoroughly?

_____

_____

_____

_____

Spotting a Counterfeit

The Son is the image of the invisible God,
the first born over all creation.
Colossians 1:15 (NIV)

Many years ago now, we took our children to Washington D.C. over their spring break. One of the sights we visited was the Bureau of Engraving and Printing. In just a 45-minute tour, we watched as they printed $162 million dollars. Not surprisingly, with all that printing, the single greatest issue that the Bureau faces is quality control. Quality control is important because counterfeiting is such a problem. The Bureau estimates that at any one time more than six billion dollars of counterfeit money is in circulation.

On the tour, our guide explained that the best way to detect counterfeit money is to compare it to the genuine article. For example, a genuine bill's portrait of the president stands out distinctly from the background, while a counterfeit portrait is lifeless and flat. Also, the saw-tooth border of the Federal Reserve and Treasury seals on a genuine bill are sharp, while on a counterfeit the saw-tooth border on the seals is blunt or uneven. The serial numbers on genuine bills are also distinctive and evenly spaced, while on a counterfeit the serial numbers may differ in color, shade, or alignment. And because comparison with the genuine article is the primary means for spotting a counterfeit, government agents spend countless hours going over every detail of the printing process and the final product.

Here's the point. Treasury agents hone their skills in recognizing fake currency, but not by studying fakes. Rather, they focus on knowing the genuine article, by which they will be able to spot counterfeits. Think about it. The number of possible variables in a counterfeit bill are limitless, which means you could never study all possible counterfeits. Wisely, the focus of Treasury agents isn't on learning an infinite number of possible fakes, but rather on memorizing the genuine article. By focusing solely and diligently on the genuine article agents are quickly able to recognize any number of counterfeits that might come their way, and the same is true spiritually! By focusing solely and diligently on Jesus, we are quickly able to recognize spiritual counterfeits.

For example, the Ebionites were a sect of Jewish Christians in the early church period, who taught that Jesus was only a man. They rejected the virgin birth and taught that Jesus was a highly moral man who kept the law. Ultimately, they believed that Jesus was an example of righteousness, an example of how each of us must live to attain salvation. Today, anyone who says that Jesus was simply an example to follow in an effort to earn salvation is a modern version of this ancient heresy. This would include Islam, which claims that Jesus was one of God's prophets, but not God himself. This would also include Buddhism and Hinduism, both of which relegate Jesus to an enlightened one, a teacher, but not God come to earth.

Of course, it was not simply a denial of Jesus' deity that spawned heresies. "Adoptionists" claimed that Jesus was human and only became the Son of God—that is divine—when he was adopted by God at his baptism.

This heresy denies the biblical account of the Christmas story, as Mary was divinely impregnated by the Holy Spirit. Docetists, on the other hand, claimed that Jesus was in no way human, but rather that he only seemed so. The word Docetism means "to seem" and they believed that all of Jesus' bodily experiences were an illusion for those watching.

The word "heresy" is derived from a Greek word that means "choice." Throughout the New Testament this Greek word is most often translated as "sect" (Acts 5:17, 15:5, 24:5 Galatians 5:20, 1 Corinthians 11:19) and describes a group that is following their own opinions about God, rather than God's revelation of himself in Scripture.

Again, there are an infinite number of potential heresies or sects. We couldn't begin to address all possible human opinion about God, just as it would be impossible to cover all possible varieties of counterfeit currency. For this reason, it is wisest to focus upon God's revelation of himself in Jesus Christ (Hebrews 12:2), by which we will be able to easily spot all spiritual counterfeits. What are

> *Treasury agents hone their skills in recognizing fake currency, but not by studying fakes. Rather, they focus on knowing the genuine article, by which they will be able to spot counterfeits.*

the distinguishing characteristics of Jesus, over and against which we are to judge all other spiritual claims? First, Jesus is the only God-Man to have ever lived, that is to say he is both fully God and fully man, fully divine and fully human. Many are willing to say that he is one or the other, but fewer will admit that he is both. Paul described him as the image of God, which is not to say he is a reflection or replica of God, but that he is God in the flesh, made available to our sight.

Paul also described him as the "firstborn over all creation," which simply means that Jesus was born. To be human one must be born. So we know that Jesus didn't simply appear, and that his body wasn't simply an illusion. Mary delivered Jesus just like all other humans are delivered after nine months of gestation. Don't be thrown by the description of Jesus as "firstborn." This isn't a designation of order. It's not that he was the first human born. This simply means that of all who have been born, Jesus is preeminent, first, supreme. Jesus, this man born to Mary, is God himself, the Creator and Sustainer of all things, who existed eternally and through whom all things are held together.

Going Deeper Questions

1. On a scale of 1 to 10, rank how easily you feel that you could be led astray by heresy. Explain why you gave yourself that ranking.

   _____

   _____

_____

_____

_____

_____

_____

_____

2. Reading Colossians 1:15-23, what about the description of Jesus provides you with greater clarity, and what provokes for you questions?

_____

_____

_____

_____

_____

_____

_____

3. What about Jesus' character and purposes do you feel you need to know better to be able to spot spiritual counterfeits?

_____

_____

_____

_____

_____

_____

_____

Good Teacher

"Good teacher," he asked, "what must
I do to inherit eternal life?" Mark 10:17 (NIV)

The question above doesn't seem to be simply an academic inquiry. Jesus was often questioned by religious leaders who were trying to trap him in his words, but that doesn't seem to be what's going on here. I say that because the man "fell on his knees before" Jesus to ask this question. He certainly could have been feigning sincerity, but it seems that this question came from a deeply emotional and personal place.

The greeting of "Good teacher" was a common greeting in that day, conveying respect and honor. The man must have seen in Jesus someone worthy of respect. He was on his knees, after all. The real question though, and the one that Jesus responds to, was directed at asking whether he saw in Jesus, goodness, even more specifically God.

"Why do you call me good?" Jesus answered. "No one is good—except God alone. Mark 10:18-19 (NIV)

Jesus was on the road to Jerusalem when he met this man. It would be his last visit to the city. There he would be crucified, giving his life as a ransom for sinners. That had been his teaching for the last three years. He taught that everyone who believes in him inherits eternal life (John 3:16), which was exactly what this man wanted.

His exact questions was "Good teacher, …what must I do to inherit eternal life?"

The common response to the greeting "Good Teacher" was something along the lines of "Most honored and good sir." That's what this man was most likely expecting to hear in Jesus' reply. In other words, this man's greeting admitted that Jesus was good, and he probably expected Jesus to return the compliment. However, Jesus responded with the question and statement, "Why do you call me good? No one is good— except God alone." In other words, I know that you recognize me as a respected teacher. I know that you want me to respond with a recognition of your goodness. But do you recognize me as God?

What do you say to a man who is expecting you to acknowledge his goodness, and who is asking about eternal life? It's a different situation altogether when someone knows they're not good. To those types, Jesus forgave them and told them to sin no more (John 8:11). But what do you say to a man who thinks he's good? Do you praise his morality? Do you celebrate his sincerity? He is, after all, on his knees. Jesus did neither of these. Jesus didn't praise the man's morality or celebrate his sincerity. Instead, Jesus quoted the law.

> You know the commandments: 'You shall not murder, you shall not commit adultery, you shall not steal, you shall not give false testimony, you shall not defraud, honor your father and mother.'"
> Mark 10:19 (NIV)

To those who thought that they were good, Jesus held up the mirror of God's law, hoping that they would see themselves as they truly were. The truth is no one is good—except God. Jesus hoped that the law would humble this man, and that he would admit his need for God's gracious forgiveness. But the man was not humbled. The man answered, "Teacher, all these I have kept since I was a boy" (Mark 10:20). Then Mark reports that...

> Jesus looked at him and loved him. "One thing you lack," he said. "Go, sell everything you have and give to the poor, and you will have treasure in heaven. Then come, follow me." At this the man's face fell. He went away sad, because he had great wealth. Mark 10:21-22 (NIV)

Jesus loved this man, and because he loved him he confronted him. Jesus candidly invited him to make up what was lacking in his goodness, by removing the one thing—his wealth—which was hindering him from following Jesus and inheriting eternal life. Jesus felt love for this man, but this man felt sadness about having to give up his wealth. Jesus felt love for this man, but this man felt love for his money, and he walked away from a relationship with God.

Did you know that it is harder for rich folks to enter heaven than for poor folks? Why is it so hard for rich folks to get into heaven? Because, we're tempted to cling to our money, rather than to follow after Jesus. Of course, the good news is that with God all things are possible and even the greediest person can be brought to a dependence upon Jesus. Make no mistake! According to Jesus, how we handle our wealth is an eternal issue. Remember, Jesus loved this man. He didn't hate this man. He loved him. He was answering the man's question. Jesus wanted him to have eternal life.

Going Deeper Questions

1. Which of the word groups below, best describes your practice and posture toward charitable giving?

   - Reluctant and resistant
   - Willing but sparingly
   - Active but not growing
   - Cheerful and growing
   - Sacrificial and generous

2. Reflecting on your answer to the question above, share with others the word group you selected above and why it best describes your posture in giving financially to support the church.

   _____

   _____

   _____

   _____

   _____

   _____

   _____

   _____

3. What steps have you taken, or can you take, to excel in the grace of giving in the next twelve months? (2 Corinthians 8:7-9)

_____
_____
_____
_____
_____
_____
_____
_____
_____
_____

4. How does it make you feel to learn that it is harder for rich people to get into heaven than for poor people?

_____
_____
_____
_____
_____
_____
_____
_____
_____
_____

Food that Spoils

Do not work for food that spoils, but for food that endures to eternal life. John 6:27 (NIV)

Jesus' miraculous feeding of 5000 people is the only miracle that is mentioned in all four gospels (Matthew 14, Mark 6, Luke 9, and John 6). A crowd followed Jesus to a lonely spot at the north end of the Sea of Galilee, far from any marketplace. As night fell, the people were hungry, and the disciples realized that they had nothing to offer them to eat. Andrew brought the contents of a little boy's lunch, five small loaves of bread and two dried fish to Jesus, and through miraculous multiplication the hungry crowd was fed, with some left over even. This so excited the crowd that they began to make plans to force Jesus to become their king. After all, if he could multiply food what more was needed to qualify him for leadership?

Of course, Jesus had no interest in political affairs and withdraw from the crowd. When the crowd found Jesus the next morning, he confronted them.

> "Do not work for food that spoils, but for food that endures to eternal life, which the Son of Man will give you. For on him God the Father has placed his seal of approval." Then they asked him, "What must we do to do the works God requires?" Jesus answered, "The work of God is this: to believe in the one he has sent." John 6:27-29 (NIV)

The feeding of 5000 was not simply meant to be a free lunch, which kept the crowd from rioting. It was meant to be a living parable, a demonstration of God's work to meet the deepest needs of humanity. Just as God physically fed the people of Israel in the wilderness by miraculously sending manna from heaven (Exodus 16), he has miraculously sent his Son from heaven to feed our souls. God in his sovereign plan had been working for thousands of years to prepare the Jews of the first century for the Messiah's arrival, and Jesus seizes the opportunity to provide lunch for 5000 people so that he can reveal himself as the Bread of Life.

How do we feed upon the Bread of Life? We feed upon the Bread of Life by expressing faith in Jesus. Jesus said, "The work of God is this: to believe in the one he has sent" (John 6:29). We "work" for food that spoils when we fail to express belief in Jesus. But we work for food that endures to eternal life, when we express faith in Jesus. The primary way we express faith in Jesus, is through obedience to his teachings. In fact, it's interesting to note that the purpose of God's provision of manna in the wilderness, his daily provision of bread for Israel, was not simply to nourish their bodies. Manna's purpose was also a means for the Israelites to express faith in God through obedience, as there were directions on how much and when they were to collect the manna (Exodus 6:5, Deuteronomy 8:3,16). The same is true today. We receive God's eternal food, when we work to express our belief in Jesus as the sent one of God, and we express our belief as we act in obedience to his teachings (John 8:51).

Are you working for food that spoils? Or are you spending your days working for food that endures to eternal life? Make no mistake, everyone eats some sort of spiritual food. We all feed our souls on something. Maybe your spiritual food is made up of activities such as gossip or worry or lust or anger. If so, then you won't have a very healthy soul.

We are all daily feeding on something, and too often we are like children whining in front of a plate of vegetables. Too often we don't want to eat what is best for us, namely obedience to Jesus' teachings. Too often we prefer the spiritual equivalent of Cheetos, rather than eating spiritual prime rib. If you find yourself spiritually famished, then a healthy diet of obedience to Jesus' teaching will strengthen you.

Going Deeper Questions

1. What activities in your life could be categorized as "working" for food that spoils?

    _____

    _____

    _____

    _____

    _____

    _____

    _____

2. What activities in your life could be categorized as "working" for food that endures to eternal life?

_____

_____

_____

_____

_____

_____

_____

3. How can you improve your spiritual diet, so that you receive more of the Bread of Life on a daily basis?

_____

_____

_____

_____

_____

_____

_____

_____

_____

Rescued by God

Who gave himself for our sins to rescue us
from the present evil age. Galatians 1:4 (NIV)

Sherri and I have three children. When our youngest, Rachel, was a little over two years old, I received a harrowing call. I was sitting in my office when the phone rang. Sherri was beside herself on the other end of the line. I heard crying in the background. It sounded like Rachel. Virtually every parent has received phone calls like this, where you know something bad has happened and you're simply waiting for the person calling to compose themselves enough to tell you the news. The waiting is torture! You want to reach into the phone and pull the news out of their throats.

The news was that Rachel had locked herself in the bathroom. Eager to be a big girl she went to the potty all by herself, closed the door for privacy, but managed to push that little button on the doorknob, which locked the bathroom door. After doing her business she was frustrated that the doorknob wouldn't turn for her so she yelled for mom to come and help, and when she realized that mom couldn't open the door either, she began to scream in panic.

Now I know what you are thinking, but the doorknob didn't have one of those tiny little key holes through which you can put a coat hanger and pop the lock open. So, there they were. Sherri was unable to force the door open and Rachel was unable to turn the knob herself.

To make matters even worse, Rachel was too immature and too panicked for a lesson in doorknob mechanics. Believe me, Sherri tried to explain to Rachel how she could rescue herself, but Rachel couldn't fully grasp the concept, nor execute the procedures needed to free herself. She was trapped.

Now the good news is that what Rachel was unable to do for herself, Sherri was able to provide for Rachel. While my two oldest children stood at the door and kept Rachel occupied, Sherri ran around the outside of the house, forced the bathroom window open, cut a hole in the screen, reached in and turned the doorknob, setting Rachel free.

> *The good news is that God has done for us what we cannot do for ourselves.*

Rachel's experience is a beautiful picture of what God offers to each of us through faith in Jesus, "who gave himself for our sins to rescue us from the present evil age" (Galatians 1:4). The question is whether we see our need for rescue. Rachel knew she needed help. She was screaming inside the bathroom asking to be rescued. Do we recognize that we are unable to provide for our own rescue, just as Rachel was unable to provide for her own rescue? The Bible teaches that we are dead in our sinfulness, unable to care for ourselves (Ephesians 2:1, Colossians 2:13). A lot of folks are not convinced that they are unable to save themselves and they spend a lot of energy on demonstrating their abilities to care for themselves spiritually

The good news is that God has done for us what we cannot do for ourselves. Through faith in Jesus, we are rescued from this present evil age. In other words, faith in Jesus frees us and we can live differently. Faith in Jesus is not simply the assurance of the forgiveness of our sin. It's that for sure. We can be confident that we are unconditionally accepted by God as we trust in Jesus' death. But faith in Jesus also provides us with the freedom needed to live differently.

How do we live differently? We live differently "in the grace of Christ" (Galatians 1:6). God rescues us from our sin because he loves us and wants to lavish his favor upon us. Just like Sherri rescued Rachel because she loved Rachel and wanted to set her free to enjoy a full and long life, God rescues us in order that we can enjoy his grace throughout life. What might it mean to "live in the grace of Christ?" It means to daily enjoy God's unmerited favor. That's what grace is, unmerited favor.

Now, would you believe that Rachel refused to come to Sherri? Sherri leaned into the bathroom through the window, but Rachel refused to be saved. She just continued to scream. I think it probably freaked her out to see her mother coming in through the window and she moved to the far side of the bathroom. If that was the only option for salvation, Rachel had no interest, and it has been my experience that some have this very response to God's offer to save us through faith in Jesus. Thankfully, once the door was unlocked by Sherri, our older kids entered the bathroom and began to comfort

Rachel. It was at that point Rachel understood that Sherri had provided for her rescue. Similarly, God has unlocked the door for us through Jesus Christ's death and resurrection. We need only to trust in his care of us by placing our faith in Jesus.

Going Deeper Questions

1. Describe your experience of being rescued by God through faith in Jesus?

   _____

   _____

   _____

   _____

2. As someone depending upon the grace of Christ, how are you living differently?

   _____

   _____

   _____

   _____

3. How might you more fully enjoy the freedom God has provided to you? (John 15:5)

   _____

   _____

   _____

   _____

An Invitation to Suffer

"If anyone would come after me, let him deny
himself and take up his cross and follow me.
John 16:24 (ESV)

Helen and Orvel Dunkeld served as missionaries in Africa for 43 years. After retiring, they worshiped at Glen Ellyn Bible Church until Helen died in 2007 at the age of 90. It was at Helen's funeral that I heard this story.

Helen and Orval went to Africa as newlyweds. The year was 1939 and Helen was only 23 years old. After some initial training in South Africa, she and Orville moved with another young couple into the Zambezi River Valley, which is in Zimbabwe. By moved, I mean they drove 1200 miles across the plateau, through open fields. There were no roads. There were no bridges. They had to forge rivers. So remote was their destination, that even the natives had a hard time surviving because of the lions, leopards, crocodiles, and malaria carrying mosquitoes.

In the Zambezi River Valley, Helen and Orville, built houses of mud bricks and thatched roofs and began to provide medical care for the locals, as well as share the gospel. The first night after their arrival a leopard broke into the yard and killed their goats, which was their only supply of milk. Over a hundred miles from the nearest village, it would be a long time before the goats were replaced. In fact, anytime they needed any supplies it took several days to make the trip to purchase what they needed, and if there was a medical crisis then you were at particular risk.

To that point, in 1959, twenty years after arriving in Africa, Helen was so tired of getting cavities and dealing with tooth aches out in the bush that during one of her visits to town she asked a dentist to pull all her teeth. The first couple of dentists refused, but she finally found one who was willing. It was at Helen's funeral that someone offered this story to describe Helen's love for God and the people of the Zambezi River Valley.

I have to admit that when I first heard that she had all her teeth pulled so that she could stay out in the bush without having to deal with cavities, I thought to myself, "A lot of older people wear dentures. That's not that big of a deal." But I was picturing Helen in her 80's, when she was retired and was attending the church regularly. But she was not an old woman when she had her teeth pulled.

If you do the math, she went to Africa at the age of 23. The year was 1939. She had her teeth pulled twenty years later in 1959, when she was only 43. More to the point, she lived to be 90, which means she had dentures longer than she had her own teeth. At the age of 43, when most folks are going through a mid-life crisis and many are having surgery to correct all types of age-related cosmetic issues, Helen was having her teeth removed so she could serve God with greater abandon and share the love of Jesus uninhibitedly with the people of Africa.

Can you imagine being so in love with God and so committed to showing his love to others that you would have your teeth yanked before you were even middle aged? Whatever our place in life, the activity of cross carrying will always involve suffering as we serve others, just as Jesus Christ served each of us by suffering on the cross.

One would think that it would be easy to recognize the crosses we are to carry, but not all suffering is cross carrying. Sometimes our suffering has little, if anything, to do with Christ. We can suffer simply because we make poor decisions, or because we are seeking personal goals that have nothing to do with building God's kingdom. Let's be honest. There are lots of activities that require self-denial but don't contribute one bit to the work of Christ in the world. Some examples of cross carrying in the suburban setting are...

- being ridiculed because you share the gospel at work or in school.
- lowering your standard of living, so that you can give more of your wealth to advance the gospel.
- spending vacation time serving in the local church or traveling to share the gospel in other parts of the world.
- serving those who can give nothing in return.

Cross carrying always involves denying ourselves in order to serve others. This does not mean that if we want something it is necessarily wrong. It means that all our desires must be submitted to Jesus' authority and purposes. Don't miss this. In the end, if there's no cross on your back, then there is not Christ in your life.

Going Deeper Questions

1. What suffering have you historically thought was cross carrying, which may not be about Christ?

   _____

   _____

   _____

   _____

   _____

2. How are you currently denying yourself in order to serve others?

   _____

   _____

   _____

   _____

3. What cross might you need to begin picking up and carrying?

   _____

   _____

   _____

   _____

   _____

Life After Birth?

For our dying bodies must be transformed into bodies that will never die; our mortal bodies must be transformed into immortal bodies. 1 Corinthians 15:53 (NLT)

Have you heard the one about the twins debating from inside their mother's womb about whether there is life after birth? It goes something like this.

"Do you believe in life after birth?" asks one of the twins to the other twin. "Yes, definitely!" answers the other twin. "This can't possibly be all there is to our existence. There has got to be a whole world beyond this experience. Why? Don't you believe in life after birth?"

"No!" the first twin answered. "All the talk about life after birth is utter nonsense! There can't be life after birth. What would that even look like?"

"I don't exactly know," answered the second twin. "But it will certainly be much better out there than in here. And I'm betting we'll actually be able to run around on our legs and eat with our mouths."

"Eat with our mouths? Why would we want to do that?" said the first twin. "That's why we have umbilical cords. What would we do with our umbilical cords if we ate with our mouths? And run? That will never happen. The umbilical cord is far too short to allow us to run!"

"We'll our bodies will be changed" answered the second twin. "Life outside the womb will be different, so our bodies will have to change too. But it will be great. All that we longed to do here, we will finally get to do out there."

"You're crazy! Where do you get those ideas? Nobody has ever come back after birth! Physical life ends with our birth and that's it! Period." insisted the first twin.

"I'll admit that I don't know the details about what life will look like after our birth. But I know that we'll get to see our mother and that she will take care of us," confessed the second twin.

"What...a Mother? You believe in a mother? Now I know you're crazy! What makes you think there's a mother? Where'd you get that idea?" asked the first twin.

"Well...here! All around us there is evidence of our mother's existence. We are alive in her and through her. Without her we would not exist!" explained the second twin.

"That's crazy! I've never noticed anything of a mother. Therefore, a mother cannot exist. All the talk of a mother is simply wishful thinking," insisted the first twin. What you consider evidence for a mother, I consider your imagination gone wild.

"Sometimes when I am really quiet," the second twin said, "you can hear her sing or feel her lovingly caresses our world! I just know that she exists."

Of course, this debate could go on and on, much like the debate that is so common about whether there is life after death. But just as we know that there is life after birth, there is also life after death. We know this because Paul describes Jesus as the "first fruits" of resurrection (1 Corinthians 15:20), which simply means Jesus was the first to be raised from the dead, after which all those who have faith in him will be raised.

Although the death rate among humanity is 100%, the good news of the gospel is that all those who have faith in Jesus will share in his physical resurrection from the dead (1 Corinthians 15:22-23). The promise of the gospel is life eternal with our Creator. What will life after death be like in heaven, with our new body? Scripture teaches that our new bodies will be imperishable, which means that all the experiences that go along with death, including disease, decay and suffering will not be a part of our experience any longer. Scripture also teaches that our new body will be a "spiritual" body.

While our natural bodies are suited for living in this world, our new body will be suited for a more spiritual experience. More to the point, Paul explained that "Flesh and blood cannot inherit the Kingdom of God" (1 Corinthians 15:50). This seems to mean that after the resurrection we will have a body perfectly suited for living in heaven. This does not mean that we will be *only* spirits—spirits do not have bodies—but that our resurrected bodies will not need physical sustenance like they do on earth (e.g. food, sleep).

We get a glimpse at what our resurrection bodies will be like when we recall Jesus' post-resurrection appearances. He still had visible wounds, and his disciples could physically touch him, yet he was able to travel effortlessly and appear and disappear at will. He could go through walls and doors. Yet, he could also eat and drink and sit and talk. Scripture tells us that our "lowly bodies" will be just "like His glorious body" (Philippians 3:21).

The gospel provides real hope not simply after death, but as we face death. We can take hope no matter what we are facing. Perhaps you're chronically ill, or even terminally ill, or maybe it's someone you love that is suffering physically. How easy it would be to live discouraged! But whatever we are facing, there is hope because Jesus has come to earth and he has overcome death. He has died for us, taking our place in death, and he overcame death through the resurrection. Though our body is laid in the grave, our mortal body will one day put on immortality and this decomposing, decaying body will become imperishable.

Going Deeper Questions

1. Considering the debate between the twins, what tempts you to doubt the reality of life after death?

   _____

   _____

2. What difficulties are you facing for which the certainty of the resurrection provides hope?

   _____

   _____

   _____

3. How might you live differently in the days ahead, because of an increased confidence in the resurrection?

   _____

   _____

   _____

My Father's Books

After that, he was seen by more than 500 of his followers at one time, most of whom are still alive, though some have died.
1 Corinthians 15:6 (NLT)

After my father died, I collected some books from his house. These particular books are important to me because they remind me of my father's antagonism toward Christianity. One of the books is titled *"Why I Am Not A Christian"* and was written by Bertrand Russell. Here are some of Russell's thoughts.

> Religion is based...mainly on fear. The whole concept of God is derived from the ancient Oriental idea of despotic rule. It is a concept quite unworthy of free men.

Russell believed emotion drives us to believe what is unreasonable, especially when it comes to religious beliefs. While I would agree with Russell to an extent, namely that emotions such as fear can drive us to believe what is unreasonable (e.g. the Boogey-Man is under my bed). It is also equally true that emotions such as fear can easily drive us away from believing what is perfectly reasonable (e.g. Jesus was raised from the dead). That was the case with my father, at least in some respects. He let fears of being considered by others as foolish drive him away from believing what is perfectly reasonable, namely that Jesus was raised from the dead.

Why is it reasonable to believe that Jesus was raised from the dead? For one, Jesus said that he would be raised, and while some have suggested that Jesus' followers made up Jesus' teachings on his resurrection (Matthew 16:21), his teachings on that subject were far too complex to manufacture. For example, Jesus said that he would destroy and rebuild the Temple in Jerusalem in just three days. Although this was initially understood by the Pharisees as a literal threat, it was latter understood rightly to be an allusion to the resurrection of Jesus' own body (John 2:19-22). Jesus also compared his resurrection to Jonah's experience of being three nights in the belly of a great fish (Matthew 12:40). While these types of allusions are expected in our modern novels, that was not the case in the ancient world. These types of allusions were far too complex for ancient literature. Instead, these teachings read much more like ancient eye-witness testimony, reported by those who heard them firsthand.

It is also improbable that Jesus' followers made up his teachings about his resurrection, because women were included as eyewitnesses. In fact, women are reported as the first people to see Jesus raised. Yet, in the first century, women were not allowed to testify in judicial proceedings. If Jesus' followers had fabricated the story of the resurrection, they would have never included women as eyewitnesses, because they would have known that including women as eyewitnesses would have undermined the credibility of the report (Matthew 28:1-10). Again, it's for this reason that many feel the reports of Jesus' resurrection read much more like eyewitness reports.

A second reason to believe that Jesus was raised from the grave is that the tomb was empty (Luke 24:1-13). Most simply put, the resurrection story would not have lasted for an hour if the emptiness of the tomb had not been established (Mark 15:42-47). Of course, the most popular explanation for the empty tomb, at least by those who doubt, is that the disciples stole the body. However, Jesus' enemies took precautions to ensure that the body wouldn't be stolen (Matthew 27:62-66). Yet, some have proposed that the disciples, although filled with fear at Jesus' arrest and crucifixion, somehow snuck up on armed soldiers, rolled a massive stone away, and stole the body (Matthew 26:56, Mark 14:51-52). This is hard to believe.

It is also hard to believe that the disciples stole the body from the tomb, because that means they later suffered and died for what they *knew* to be a hoax. Follow me here. Lots of people suffer and die for what they *believe* to be true. But no one, in their right mind, suffers and dies for what they *know* to be a lie.

Realizing that no one suffers and dies for what they know to be untrue, some have proposed that Jesus really didn't die at all.

> *The truth is that our emotions can drive us to believe what is unreasonable (e.g. the Boogey-Man is under our bed), as well as drive us away from believing what is perfectly reasonable (e.g. God raised Jesus from the dead).*

Known as the "swoon" theory, some in the last few hundred years have suggested that Jesus was simply unconscious. However, this notion has most likely grown in popularity over the last couple of hundred years, only because anyone who had witnessed a Roman crucifixion would have quickly dismissed swooning as a real possibility. For Jesus to have escaped the tomb on his own means he would have rolled away a giant stone all by himself, while in complete darkness, and after having been flogged, hung on a cross for six hours, with nails driven through his feet and hands, and stabbed in the side with a spear. This theory is weak because Romans were skilled executioners, who made sure Jesus was dead (John 19:31-34).

Another reason to believe that Jesus was raised is that the Apostles were dramatically changed after the resurrection. Even when imprisoned and beaten, the Apostles ignored the warnings of Jewish leaders and continued to proclaim that Jesus had been raised (Acts 5:29-42). Only seeing Jesus raised would explain how previously cowardly men would have suddenly become courageous. And it was not only those who had been closest to Jesus who were changed. People like Saul were changed too (Acts 7-9). Later known as the Apostle Paul, Saul was at one time a Jewish leader committed to wiping out the followers of Jesus. Saul was changed though after seeing the raised Jesus himself and he went on to suffer for preaching about the resurrection of Jesus. Finally, Paul reported that over 500 saw Jesus alive (1 Corinthians 15:5-6). This is no small matter, as Paul was basically saying, "If you don't believe me, talk to the others who saw him."

My father died at age 67, but not before believing that Jesus was raised. Faith in Jesus' resurrection is not simply a myth created to console us as we face death, as Bertrand Russell insisted, but rather the reasonable conclusion based upon strong evidence. Dad's books sit on a shelf in my office as a reminder that there are good reasons to believe that Jesus was raised from the dead.

Going Deeper Questions

1. Rank your confidence in the resurrection of Jesus on a scale of 1-10. Why did you give yourself the ranking that you did?

    _____
    _____
    _____

2. What questions do you have unanswered about the resurrection?

    _____
    _____
    _____
    _____

3. With whom can you share the reasons for believing in Jesus' resurrection?

    _____
    _____
    _____
    _____

Forest Gump Faith

Be afraid of the One who can destroy
both soul and body in hell. Matthew 10:28 (NIV)

Writing for *Entertainment Weekly*, Jeff Gordinier noted that "pop culture is going gaga for spirituality." However, he also noted that people are self-serving in their theological selections. He wrote:

> Seekers of the day are apt to peel away the tough theological stuff and pluck out the most dulcet elements of faith, coming up with a soothing sampler of Judeo-Christian imagery, Eastern meditation, self-help lingo, a vaguely conservative craving for 'virtue,' and a loopy New Age pursuit of 'peace.' This happy free-for-all, appealing to Baptists and stargazers alike, comes off more like Forest Gump's ubiquitous 'boxa chocolates' than like any real belief.

It's fascinating to read in a secular magazine a criticism of modern spirituality. By "boxa chocolates" Gordinier is referencing the tendency to embrace only those theological truths that taste good to us, much like people are apt to do when given a box of assorted chocolates. Among assorted theological issues, the certainty of Hell is often one of the most offensive Christian doctrines. If you share your faith regularly then at some point you are bound to hear the question, "How can a loving God send people to Hell?"

We don't like the idea of Hell, but it is important to realize that the reality of Hell is taught throughout the New Testament. The Apostle Paul wrote that those who do not obey the gospel "…will be punished with everlasting destruction" (2 Thessalonians 1:9). And in John's book of Revelation we read that some are cast for eternity into the Lake of Fire (Revelation 20:13-15). Perhaps even more noteworthy are Jesus' teachings on Hell. Jesus proclaimed that anyone who says to their brother "You fool!" will be in danger of the fire of hell (Matthew 5:22). And, in teaching on the drastic measures we should take to avoid sin, we are to even pluck out our eyes if they cause us to lust or cut off our hand if it causes us to sin. He said, "It is better for you to lose one part of your body than for your whole body to be thrown into hell" (Matthew 5:30). And when commissioning his disciples on a short-term mission trip, and warning them that they will meet with persecution along the way, he said:

> Do not be afraid of those who kill the body but cannot kill the soul. Rather, be afraid of the One who can destroy both soul and body in hell. Matthew 10:28 (NIV)

In describing hell, Jesus labeled it as a place "where the fire never goes out" (Mark 9:43), and where the "worm does not die" (Mark 9:49), a place of unspeakable suffering. Finally, a vivid portrait of suffering in hell is provided in Jesus' story of the Rich Man and Lazarus (Luke 16:19-31).

The short of it is that the reality of hell is taught throughout the New Testament, which means to selectively dismiss these teachings is to do so at our own peril. After all, it's the bad news of our sin leading to condemnation in Hell that makes the good news of God's forgiveness through faith in Jesus so appealing!

Going Deeper Questions

1. What has been your historic disposition/belief about the certainty of coming judgment and the reality of Hell?

   _____

   _____

   _____

2. In what ways is it both challenging and inspiring to learn that the certainty of judgement and the reality of Hell is taught throughout the New Testament?

   _____

   _____

   _____

3. How might you live differently in the days ahead because of the certainty of judgment and the reality of Hell?

   _____

   _____

   _____

Wonderful Counselor

He will be called Wonderful Counselor, Mighty God,
Everlasting Father, Prince of Peace. Isaiah 9:6 (NIV)

There are times in life when you need an expert, when you want the comfort of knowing that you are getting the very best possible advice. Many years ago, I remember being in just that type of situation. My family had been invited to a friend's house for dinner. We were scrambling to get out the door, when Rachel, our youngest child, complained about her ear hurting. She was only two at the time. We didn't think much of, but on the way out the door we grabbed the children's Tylenol bottle and threw it in the diaper bag.

After dinner that evening, the adults were sitting around talking while the kids played together, when I noticed Rachel was walking around the house with her pacifier in her mouth—which meant she had been in her diaper bag and that she had probably emptied the contents of the diaper bag all over the floor in order to find her pacifier. I got up from talking with the adults to go clean up the mess.

Sure enough, the contents of the diaper bag were all over the floor, and right in the middle of the mess was the children's Tylenol bottle, with the lid off. There wasn't a pill anywhere to be found. As I'm standing in the foyer with the bottle cap in one hand and the empty bottle in the other, stunned by what this probably meant, Rachel walked in from the other room looked up at me and announced "I ate it!" "You what?" I asked.

Of course Sherri and I had no idea how many pills were left in the bottle and Rachel was certainly no help in estimating the number she had eaten, except that when she opened her mouth there was pink residue all over the inside of her cheeks. It was at that point we decided to call Poison Control, and I can't tell you how badly I wanted to speak with an expert.

As I dialed the phone, I thought to myself if the person who answers gives me any cause to doubt their counsel, I'm going straight to the Emergency Room. Poison control was great! They said that for her weight and age she could eat as many as 28 children's tablets and she'd be fine. It was a 30 tablet bottle though. We later found one tablet on the floor, and we knew that we had dosed out of that bottle before. So Sherri and I rested easy.

There are times in life when you want the best counsel possible and that is how Jesus is described. 700 years before Jesus' birth, Isaiah announced him as the Wonderful Counselor, which reveals his character as well as his ministry to us. Isaiah originally spoke these words as a prophecy during the reign of King Ahaz, who led Israel from about 740-700 B.C. The Old Testament book of 2 Kings offers a short biography of Ahaz that includes details of his 1) remodeling the Temple in Jerusalem in order to better suit pagan worship, and 2) confiscating the gold and the silver from God's Temple in order to send it off as a gift to the Assyrian king in an attempt to buy his protection, and 3) offering his son as a sacrifice to pagan gods in an attempt to enlist their protection (2 Kings 16). Against this backdrop, Isaiah tells of God's coming judgement, but also of God's coming counselor.

Do you feel "lost," unsure of what to do next, or of how to make your way through life? Jesus is *the* Wonderful Counselor. The word "wonderful" literally means "wonder," as in supernatural. In other words, it's not simply that this child's counsel will be "terrific," but that *he* is miraculous. The point is that the counsel this child offers will be out of this world. He is a wonder of a counselor, a miraculous counselor.

Of course, Jesus' birth was supernatural, born to a virgin, who conceived him by the Holy Spirit's intervention. Beyond his conception, Jesus also turned water into wine, healed lepers, made the blind see and the lame walk. He walked on water, multiplied bread to feed 5000, and he raised the dead. He was also raised from the dead himself. If you've ever shopped for a counselor, then you know that you want someone who can sympathize with the troubles you are facing. The problem is you don't simply want someone with whom you can cry. You also want someone who has overcome, someone who has faced what you are struggling with and has conquered it. You want an expert, and there is only one person who can claim to both understand the sin problem that humanity faces and who has overcome it—Jesus. When it comes to dealing with sin and the darkness it causes there is only one expert. There is only one person who is truly wonderful. Jesus said of himself...

> "I am the light of the world. If you follow me, you won't be stumbling through the darkness, because you will have the light that leads to life." John 8:12 (NIV)

When we are looking for wisdom and insight into the darkened heart of mankind there is no one more qualified than Jesus, no one more compassionate than Jesus, and no one more capable to provide the remedy.

Going Deeper Questions

1. Isaiah presents the birth of Jesus as the answer to all earthly troubles (Isaiah 9:6). What substitutes for Jesus' Wonderful Counsel do people offer?

   _____

   _____

   _____

   _____

2. When do you seek the "counsel" of Jesus? How have you found Jesus' counsel to be "wonderful"?

   _____

   _____

   _____

   _____

   _____

   _____

3. On what issues/situations do you currently need Jesus' counsel?

   _____

   _____

   _____

   _____

On God's Fairness and Our Finiteness

Surely I spoke of things I did not understand,
things too wonderful for me to know. Job 42:3 (NIV)

The year was 1945, and at the ripe old age of only 27 Billy Graham was already crisscrossing the country, filling auditoriums and speaking to crowds as large as 30,000. At that time, Graham was a full-time evangelist for an organization called Youth for Christ, and his reputation was growing like the crowds that came to listen to him. Of course, the rest is history. Graham served faithfully in ministry for more than 70 years.

But did you know that Graham wasn't the only evangelist packing auditoriums in 1945? Furthermore, did you know that he wasn't even considered the best evangelist at that time? It's a little-known fact, but two other men were far better known and considered by many to be far more promising as evangelists than Graham. Their names were Chuck Templeton and Bron Clifford.

All three men were in their mid to late twenties, but Templeton and Clifford were preaching more than Graham, and filling larger stadiums. One seminary president, after hearing Chuck Templeton preach called him "the most gifted and talented young preacher in America today." And in 1946, the National Association of Evangelicals published an article on men who were being "best used of God" within that organization's work and the article highlighted Chuck Templeton's ministry. It didn't even mention Billy Graham. Why isn't Chuck Templeton's name a household name like Graham's?

Graham and Templeton met in 1945 and became fast friends. Both preached with Youth for Christ, but Templeton later settled down to pastor a church that grew quickly to average over 1200 in Sunday attendance. But in 1950, just five years after beginning in the ministry, Templeton left it all and returned to pursue his original career as a radio and television commentator and a newspaper columnist. His faith had been completely sidetracked. In fact, Templeton went from preaching throughout Europe and leading a large church, to atheism—denying the very existence of God.

As Templeton described it, one day he was reading *Time* magazine and there was an article with pictures in it of African children who were starving to death because of a severe drought. The article and pictures caused such a crisis of faith for him that he could no longer believe that God is good, or even exists for that matter. In his search for answers, Templeton went on to write several books, one of which was titled, "Farewell to God: My Reasons for Rejecting the Christian Faith."

In rejecting Christianity, Templeton explained that it doesn't seem that God is fair in his dealings with humanity, namely in allowing children to starve to death. Those who have Templeton's doubts often cite stories from the Old Testament that call into question God's fairness, stories such as Noah's flood, the destruction of Sodom and Gomorrah, as well as the destruction of Jericho and other Canaanite cities. How can a good God order the destruction of entire populations, which included children?

The best answer to the question of God's fairness in allowing people to suffer must address the reality with which we all struggle, a finite perspective. The short of it is that we are limited in our understanding, which is not to say that we know nothing, but rather that we cannot possibly expect to understand all of God's actions. Because we can't understand all of God's actions, we must trust in God's character.

For example, we know from Scripture that God is "merciful and gracious...slow to anger and rich in unfailing love and faithfulness" (Exodus 34:6). And, in the book of Ezekiel, we learn that God takes, "no pleasure in the death of the wicked, but that the wicked turn from his way and live" (Ezekiel 33:11).

> *The short of it is that we are limited in our understanding, which is not to say that we know nothing, but rather that we cannot possibly expect to understand all of God's actions.*

The truth is that God waits patiently before executing judgment, wanting none to perish but all to come to repentance. For example, we shouldn't forget Noah's preaching to those same people whom God later swept away in the flood (2 Peter 2:5). We also shouldn't forget God's posture in destroying Sodom and Gomorrah, giving assurance to Abraham that if there were only ten righteous persons in the city they would not be destroyed (Genesis 18:32). And when we consider God's command to the Israelites to wipe out every man, woman and child among the Canaanites, we shouldn't forget God's patience, waiting 400 years before executing his judgment (Genesis 15:12-14, 16). We see this same patience shown toward Rahab in Jericho's destruction, as well as in Nineveh, as the city repents of their sin. Even today, we know that God delays the return of Christ so that more people may come to repentance (2 Peter 3:9).

While we cannot understand fully God's actions, we are comforted to know God's character. He is patient, slow to anger, abounding in love and ready to receive and pardon the repentant.

Going Deeper Questions

1. When and why have you questioned God's fairness, whether towards you or others?

_____

_____

_____

_____

_____

_____

_____

_____

_____

_____

_____

2. How have you answered those questions of fairness, and resolved those feelings of unfair treatment? Or, how do you continue to struggle with questions of unfairness and feelings of unfair treatment?

_____

_____

_____

_____

_____

_____

_____

_____

_____

_____

_____

3. How is the Scriptural call to repentance both comforting and challenging?

_____

_____

_____

_____

_____

_____

_____

_____

_____

Written *For* Us, But Not *To* Us

All Scripture is God-breathed and is useful
for teaching, rebuking, correcting and training in righteousness.
2 Timothy 3:16 (NIV)

Ever had the experience of accidentally reading someone else's mail? You go to your mailbox, pull out the letters, open and begin reading them, only to realize that the mailman put someone else's mail in your mailbox. The first clue that you're reading someone else's mail is that you don't recognize any of the names or references. That's inevitably our experience when reading the Bible, because it wasn't written to us. A common mistake made when reading the Bible is to think that it was written to us. It's true to say that the Bible was written *for* us, that God intended for us to read Scripture, but it was not written *to* us. Thinking that the Bible was written to us would be like opening someone else's mail and expecting to understand all that was written there.

To make matters even worse, the Bible was written not to my neighbor, with whom I share a common language and culture, but to a people who lived thousands of years ago and in a faraway land. To drive the point home, I've included a small portion from a letter written in 1926 to my Grandmother. She lived in rural west Texas less than one hundred years ago.

The fall wheat made a little over 2300 bushels and the bound and headed oats about the same. I don't think the headed oats realy mack that much for

161

they was damp in the shock. The jersey looks very
well. She gets her head in the oats when we are
feeding the horses. Bill and Rachel are going to
school. Bill rides the little bay. The one I traded to
Verg. I bought a roan horse. Inez and Rachel rides
him.

So much in this letter is nonsensical to me. I don't
know whether to feel sorry for Bill because he's having to
ride a "bay" to school or to be glad for him. I don't know
if Verg is a bad horse trader or a good one, and who
knows if 2300 bushels is a good fall crop. But, because I
realize that the letter wasn't written to me, I'm less
frustrated and I recognize the work that will be necessary
to understand its message. I realize that I'm going to have
to do some research about life in rural west Texas if I'm
going to understand what was written to my Granny.

Similarly, it's important for us to understand that
the Bible's ancient authors wrote to ancient audiences,
and that the names of people and places, as well as
descriptions of events, are going to be foreign to us and
will require work if we are going to understand them. This
means that the Bible is not a miracle book in the sense
that ancient authors wrote to modern audiences. The
Bible is a miracle book in that God spoke through ancient
authors to ancient audiences and its message is still
speaking today. All of Scripture is God-breathed and
useful for teaching, rebuking, correcting and training in
righteousness, and it's our job to work to understand the
message from the ancient authors to the ancient
audiences.

This work of getting to know the author and audience will require language and grammar studies, as well as a knowledge of ancient history and culture. Once the message of Scripture is understood in its original context, then a bridge can be built for application to our modern lives. Most biblical commentaries offer some explanation of these background issues in their effort to interpret and apply Scripture. As we do this work, there is a wealth of wisdom and strength waiting for us. Look at what God said about his Word through Isaiah.

> The rain and snow come down from the heavens and stay on the ground to water the earth. They cause the grain to grow, producing seed for the farmer and bread for the hungry. It is the same with my word. I send it out, and it always produces fruit. It will accomplish all I want it to, and it will prosper everywhere I send it. Isaiah 55:10-11 (NLT)

The imagery here is of God sending his Word to water our lives, in much the same way rain waters the earth. God's Word always produces fruit, which means that it always accomplishes its transforming work in our lives. For this reason, King David wrote, "I have hidden your word in my heart, so that I might not sin against you" (Psalm 119:11). King David used Scripture to insulate his life against sinful behaviors and attitudes, because he knew that it brings God's transforming presence and power into his life.

Going Deeper Questions

1. What have you historically believed about the nature of Scripture?

   _____

   _____

   _____

   _____

2. When and how have you experienced the "living and active" power of Scripture? (Hebrews 4:12)

   _____

   _____

   _____

   _____

3. What are your current habits of reading, meditating and memorizing Scripture?

   _____

   _____

   _____

   _____

4. How might you strengthen your habits of studying Scripture in order to experience more of its usefulness in your life?

   _____

   _____

   _____

   _____

Rainbows and Relationships

You intended to harm me, but God intended it for good to accomplish what is now being done, the saving of many lives.
Genesis 50:20 (NIV)

Did you know that rainbows are not half circles? The perceived shape of a rainbow depends upon your perspective. Rainbows result when sunlight is bent as it passes through raindrops, and they occur most often when the sun is between 40 and 42 degrees above the horizon. From an airplane though, it is possible to see the full circle of a rainbow because there are raindrops above and below the observer. On the ground we look up to see the rainbow as the raindrops fall towards us, but when one is high above the ground it is possible to see raindrops both falling toward us and away from us and the refraction of the light forms a full circle. Imagine Noah, seeing the full circle of a rainbow from mount Ararat, after the flood waters had receded (Genesis 8:4, 9:13)

Learning that I most often only see half of a rainbow, because of my vantage point, reminds me of the difference between my perspective and God's perspective on the events of life. At all times, God sees the completed reality of his work of redemption in the world, while we can only see some of that reality. Joseph believed in God's good purposes despite the evil he had experienced in life, and it made all the difference in his relationships. Joseph was able to forgive those who had harmed him, because he was able to see the full picture of God's good work despite the evil in the world.

Joseph's story is one of God's work to preserve a family despite their sinfulness. Jacob had twelve sons, of whom his favorite was Joseph. Jacob's favoritism toward Joseph, combined with Joseph's self-serving behavior, created a rift in his relationship with his eleven brothers. Fueled by hate, Joseph's brothers sold him into slavery, and he was carted off to Egypt. God blessed Joseph in Egypt though, and he was elevated to the position of second in command, a position from which he served the nation by leading them through a severe famine. The famine was so widespread that even Jacob's family had to come from Canaan to buy food in Egypt, and in so doing Joseph was reunited with his brothers.

While it is certainly impressive that Joseph forgave his brothers, what is most instructive is the reason he gave for forgiving them.

While it is certainly impressive that Joseph forgave his brothers for their evil against him, what is most instructive is the reason he gave for forgiving them. Joseph said of his brothers' sinful actions toward him, "You intended to harm me, but God intended it for good to accomplish what is now being done, the saving of many lives" (Genesis 50:20). Joseph saw life's events, even the evil experiences in the world, from God's perspective, and it enabled him to extend forgiveness to his brothers and experience restoration in his relationships with them.

Of course, just because God intends to use the evil actions of humanity for his good purposes, does not mean that we should participate in evil. What it means is that where "sin increased, grace abounded all the more" (Romans 5:20). It means that no amount of evil has, or will, ever overcome God's work of redemption in the world. The Apostle Paul famously said about life's difficulties that "what is seen is temporary, but what is unseen is eternal" (2 Corinthians 4:16-18). Can we see the unseen real? Can we see the reality of a full circle rainbow, even when evil is present in the world?

All my life my vision was perfect, but at the ripe old age of 44 my arms were suddenly too short for reading and no light was quite bright enough. Just as our vision can suffer physically, it can also suffer spiritually. Joseph fixed his eyes on the good purposes of God. That's faith, and it enabled Joseph to forgive his brothers and be restored to them.

So, what are we to do? We are to forgive, just as Joseph did. We are to forgive just as we have been forgiven through faith in Jesus Christ. The Apostle Paul wrote, "Bear with each other and forgive whatever grievances you may have against one another. Forgive as the Lord forgave you" Colossians 3:13 (NIV).

Going Deeper Questions

1. Joseph believed that God overcame the evil perpetrated against him (Genesis 50:20). On a scale of one to ten, how confident are you that this is the case in your life? Give examples.

_____

_____

_____

_____

2. How do the following Scriptures support Joseph's view that God is working for our good? (Romans 8:18-39, 2 Corinthians 4:16-18, James 1:2-4)

_____

_____

_____

_____

3. How have you seen God bring good out of the harm others have done to you or those you love?

_____

_____

_____

_____

4. Joseph not only expressed his forgiveness, but also showed his brothers forgiveness (Genesis 50:21). How do you do at both expressing and demonstrating your forgiveness toward others?

_____

_____

_____

_____

Spiritual Paupers

Praise be to the God and Father of our Lord Jesus Christ,
who has blessed us in the heavenly realms with every spiritual
blessing in Christ. Ephesians 1:3 (NIV)

When Hetty Green died in 1916, at the age of 82, she was described as "America's Greatest Miser." Strangely enough though, she left an estate valued at over 100 million dollars in cash to her two children, Ned and Sylvia. In today's dollars, that would be over $2.2 Billion. Although one of the richest women in the history of the world, she lived as if she was poor. She wore only black clothing, because it didn't show as much dirt and required less washing, and she did her own laundry. She ate cold oatmeal every day for breakfast, because it cost money to heat the oatmeal, and she rarely turned on the heat in her house. She walked to the grocery store, and at the grocery store she bought broken cookies in bulk, because they were considerably less expensive than whole cookies. She would also return her berry boxes to the grocery store for a nickel each.

Of course, much of this behavior could be seen as harmless and eccentric. But that was not always the case. Her son, Ned, had to have one of his legs amputated, because Hetty was so intent on finding a free clinic for his treatment that the delay in getting him help allowed an infection to spread. Hetty Green was wealthy but acted like a pauper. She lived as if she was without any resources, when the truth was that she was one of the wealthiest people who has ever lived.

Unfortunately, Hetty's lifestyle is like the spiritual experience of far too many Christians. Christians can often live as if they are spiritual paupers, when in reality we have inherited the wealth of heaven. Paul wrote that through faith in Jesus Christ we have been given every spiritual blessing in the heavenly realms (Ephesians 1:3).

Of course, this does not mean that life will be easy for Christians. In fact, Paul wrote the letter to the Ephesians from a Roman jail cell, while awaiting his trial before Caesar. Life will not be easy for Christians, but too often we make it unnecessarily hard because we do not enjoy the spiritual blessings that are ours. Too often we live as spiritual paupers when we have inherited the wealth of heaven.

How do we access our spiritual blessings? We access our blessings through the Spirit (Ephesians 1:13-14). That makes sense. Right? Spiritual blessings are accessed through the Spirit. In other words, Paul is not encouraging the Christians in Ephesus to simply think differently about themselves or their situation, although God's Word will certainly change the way we think about ourselves and the world in which we live. Paul was saying that we factually possess God's presence in our lives through faith in Jesus and that we have access to our spiritual blessings because of the Spirit, who is with us.

Imagine the moment when Ned and Sylvia Green were physically handed their mother's bankbooks, which gave them immediate access to all their mother's money. Through faith in Jesus' death, we have become the beneficiaries of God, granting us immediate access to the wealth of heaven through the presence of the Spirit.

The question is, how do we live differently in order to enjoy more of our spiritual blessings? The answer is that we must be "filled with the Spirit." Paul wrote in the book of Ephesians,

> Do not get drunk on wine, which leads to debauchery. Instead, be filled with the Spirit.
> Ephesians 5:18 (NIV)

Paul is very clear. There is an interplay between our physical actions and our enjoying our spiritual blessings. Simply put, our spiritual blessings become earthly realities, as we increasingly participate in Spirit led physical activities. This is how God has designed the world, giving us physical bodies by which we can participate in spiritual realities. The most obvious example was seen in the physical birth, life, death, and resurrection of Jesus Christ, which through faith now provides us access to all our spiritual blessings.

Unfortunately, we too often believe that spiritual activities most closely resemble magic, requiring secret words (e.g., abracadabra) and mysterious symbols. To some degree, the Church has even fostered this misperception, making the interplay between our physical activities and our spiritual blessings far too complex. The truth is that our spiritual blessings are experienced through some mundane and even routine physical activities. Below are some examples of physical activities, identified by Paul in the letter to the Ephesians, which help us more thoroughly enjoy the blessings that are ours through faith in Jesus.

171

- Prayer (Ephesians 1:15-23, 3:14-19, 6:18).
- Putting off sinful behavior and putting on righteous behavior (Ephesians 4:17-5:14)
- Speaking to one another through psalms, hymns, and spiritual songs (Ephesians 5:15-19)
- Submitting to one another out of reverence for Christ (Ephesians 5:21-6:9)
- Wearing the full armor of God (Ephesians 6:10-18)

These types of activities cause the spiritual blessings that are already ours to flow more freely into our lives. It would be like Hetty Green's children physically going to the bank for the first time to make a withdrawal. Blessings such as love, joy, peace, patience, kindness, goodness, faithfulness, gentleness, and self-control become an experienced reality in our lives as we act according to the Spirit (Galatians 5:22-23).

Going Deeper Questions

1. What do you imagine it was like to live with Hetty Green?

   _____

   _____

   _____

   _____

2. What do you imagine it was like to inherit the wealth of Hetty Green?

_____

_____

_____

_____

3. What spiritual blessings are you daily enjoying, and what blessings of the Spirit do you want to enjoy in the days ahead more thoroughly?

_____

_____

_____

_____

_____

_____

_____

4. Which of the Spirit led activities listed are you participating in regularly, and which might you practice more often? And how might practicing these activities enrich your life?

_____

_____

_____

_____

_____

_____

_____

Bridling the Beast

If anyone considers himself religious and yet does not keep a tight
rein on his tongue, he deceives himself and his religion is worthless.
James 1:26 (NIV)

Do you remember the Litmus paper from high
school chemistry class? Litmus paper is that little thin strip
of paper, which when dunked into a Petri dish full of
water changes colors, depending upon the acidity or
alkalinity of the water. The role of Litmus paper is to give
a clear indication of the water's PH (i.e., potential of
hydrogen), which helps chemists identify the purity of a
particular water sample and know how to best treat the
water's impurities.

Did you know that there is a Litmus test for
religious practice? We can gain an indication as to whether
we are living God-honoring lives simply by testing
whether we have a tight rein on our tongue. James wrote,

> If anyone considers himself religious and yet does
> not keep a tight rein on his tongue, he deceives
> himself and his religion is worthless. James 1:26
> (NIV)

Imagine going through all the religious ritual of
regular attendance at church, or giving your money to
advance the Kingdom of God, or participating in a small
group or in mission trips, only to learn that your religion
was worthless because you failed to rein in your tongue.
How could this be the case? According to James, a God-

honoring life will always include control of our tongue.

Reins work in controlling a horse by placing pressure on the mouth, tongue and jaw of the horse. Keeping a "tight rein" means keeping a lot of pressure on the jaw of the horse. To run, a horse needs the freedom to lower his head, but pulling firmly on the reins places pressure on the mouth and tongue, forcing the horse to raise his head, a position from which he cannot run.

In college, I spent several summers at an outdoor education camp, which was located in the north woods of Wisconsin. There I served as a camp counselor to twelve year-old boys. When not leading programs though, I would often sneak off to the barn to see the horses. They had several different types of horses at the camp, some for riding

> *We are not saved by keeping a tight rein on our tongue. We are saved by God's grace apart from anything we do (Ephesians 2:8-9). But those who are being saved will keep a tight rein on their tongue.*

and others for work. The work horses were giant Belgian horses. Averaging over 2000 lbs., the Belgians were used in the summer to pull kids around camp on hayrides. In the winter they would pull sleighs through the snow. To give you a sense of their power, Belgians can pull a wagon, fully loaded with campers, up a hill without any wheels on the wagon. In other words, they could drag a full wagon uphill.

On occasion, when the Belgians were not working, we would take them swimming, which meant riding them bareback (i.e., no saddle) and without any reins, down to the lake. Those horses loved swimming! Like the cowboy I always wanted to be, I would jump on the back of one of those huge horses, and we would walk them out of the corral. Bear in mind that the back of these horses was so broad that one's legs only went about halfway down the side of the horse. In other words, there was no real way of holding on. You couldn't lock your heels under the belly of the horse. You just sat on top.

Once outside the corral though, and without any reins mind you, these giant horses would immediately start trotting. They knew where they were going, and they were eager to get there. For those who have never ridden a horse, trotting is a terribly uncomfortable gate, and without a saddle or reins it is almost impossible to stay on top of the horse because the bouncing is so violent. Thankfully, the closer we came to the lake, the horses broke into a full gallop, which is a much smoother ride. All I could do at that point was dig my heels into the horse's ribs as tightly as possible and grab two handfuls of hair on the mane. My goal was to hold on until we got to the water, at which point it would be safe to fall off the back of the horse. The problem was that when the lake came into view the horse broke into a full sprint, and the inside of my legs were cramping from digging my heels into the horse's side. Thankfully, the next thing I felt was the cold wetness of the lake. Once we were in the water together, I slid off the horse's back and held onto his neck as the horse swam. It was a powerful experience.

Without any reins, I was completely at the mercy of that massive animal. My efforts to control or direct the horse were worthless, and that is what James says about a person who fails to keep a tight rein on their tongue. Their religion is worthless. Make sure to understand. We are not saved by keeping a tight rein on our tongue. We are saved by God's grace apart from anything that we do (Ephesians 2:8-9). But those who are being saved will keep a tight rein on their tongue. They will work hard to bridle the beast, because they want to honor God with their lives.

Why is the tongue so central to our lives as worshippers of God? Our tongues are central to our lives as worshippers because it reflects what is in our heart. Jesus himself said, "the mouth speaks what the heart is full of" (Matthew 12:34). If we were to take inventory of all that we say in a single day, what might we find is in our heart?

Going Deeper Questions

1. On a scale of one to ten, how well are you doing at controlling your tongue? Give examples.

    _____

    _____

    _____

    _____

    _____

    _____

    _____

    _____

2. Describe a time when a failure to keep your tongue under control had a negative impact on your life. (Proverbs 18:21)

_____

_____

_____

_____

_____

_____

_____

3. What correlation do you find between the spiritual condition of your heart, and how you are using your tongue? (James 3:9-12)

_____

_____

_____

_____

4. How might we address the spiritual condition of our heart in order to correct what is coming out of our mouths? (Matthew 15:1-20)

_____

_____

_____

_____

_____

_____

_____

The Merciful and Mercy

Blessed are the merciful, for they will be shown mercy.
Matthew 5:7 (NIV)

In my second year of graduate school at Wheaton College, I took a spiritual formation class focused on curriculum design and assessment. Halfway through the semester the teacher divided the class into groups and gave each group the assignment of writing a creative lesson using a Biblical passage and then teaching that lesson to the class. When the day came for my group to present our topic we had a simple lesson, but one that we thought was creative. We had three goals. We wanted the class to…

1. Listen as we read to them a parable.
2. Walk together, across the campus, giving the students time and space to think about the application of the parable to their lives.
3. Discuss the parable's application together.

After reading the parable to the class, we left the classroom and set out for a walk across campus. The walk was to be less than one hundred yards in length, as we were only moving from the building in which our class met to the student center. During the walk the students were to begin identifying points of application from the parable for their lives. The problem was that the minute we stepped out of the building and into the open air a man approached our group and began to beg for money.

He smelled. His clothes were tattered, and his hair was unkempt. Every now and then the college had vagrants wander onto campus and harass the students by begging for money, and this guy certainly fit the bill. As one of the leaders of the lesson I was the first out the doors and the first approached. "No," I said politely but firmly and moved on, knowing that if I stopped to help the whole group would be distracted from the lesson.

Passing him quickly, I looked over my shoulder to see if he was going to speak to anyone else, and he was intent on begging from everyone who came out the door. One after another, he asked everyone in our class for money. He said he needed help with train fare, but he didn't smell like he would use the money to buy a train ticket. When it became apparent to him that my classmates were not going to be easily persuaded to stop and help, he became much more insistent. "God," he said at the top of his lungs, "I thought this was supposed to be a Christian college, like a church or something." He even grabbed one of the men in the group by the shirtsleeve to try and slow him down a little, but the fellow jerked away.

It was at that point, when things started to get a little tense, that the professor stepped in. Politely, but with great authority, the professor said, "Look here, you can't be begging on campus, and if you continue to bother us then I will call security." With that the beggar slipped away. By this time though, we were halfway to our destination and the group was completely distracted. No one was talking about the parable that we had read to them. Honestly, it was probably the furthest thing from their mind.

Instead, everyone was talking about how irritating the beggar had been. I heard one woman say from the back of the group, "I'm ok with someone asking once, but to ask again and again is so rude. What does he think 'no' means anyway?" With that phrase still hanging in the air we stepped into the college's student center, and I directed the students in our class to find a seat.

The class was all stirred up from the episode with the beggar, so we thought it would be wise to begin the final phase of our lesson by re-reading the parable before attempting to lead any discussion on our topic. I opened my Bible and reread to the class the parable of The Good Samaritan (Luke 10:25-37). *That's right, the same parable that I had read to them not five minutes earlier.*

If you are familiar with this story, then you know it is the story of one man stopping to help another who is in need. The Biblical topic that my group had selected for our lesson was mercy, and as I finished reading that parable, now for a second time, the class was silent. It was dawning on them that the walk itself had little to do with the learning process that evening, while the person we met along the walk had everything to do with the lesson.

We had hired an actor to dress up as a beggar and harass the class, and no one had stopped to help him. No one had shown him any mercy. After hearing what is arguably one of the best-known stories on mercy in the entire Bible, these ministry graduate students had blown right by someone needing mercy. Now, the point was not that we must help everyone who asks us for money. The point was rather how tremendously difficult it is to get biblical knowledge from our head to our heart.

None of the 25 ministry minded students, good Christian men and women who were committed to a lifetime of professional soul care, had stopped to even listen to the man's story, or try and encourage him, or to offer to pray with him. Yet Jesus said, "Blessed are the merciful, for they will be shown mercy" (Matthew 5:7). What are we to make of our struggle to show others mercy, when we each so desperately want to receive mercy from God? Ironically, the inability to show others mercy, is one indication of our desperate need for God's mercy.

Going Deeper Questions

1. Take time to read the parable of The Parable of the Good Samaritan (Luke 10:25-37). What are some elements of the story that stand out to you?

   _____

   _____

   _____

   _____

2. Why do you think that the students in my class failed to stop and help the beggar?

   _____

   _____

   _____

   _____

   _____

   _____

   _____

3. Why do you think those who passed by the victim in the parable refused to stop?

_____

_____

_____

_____

_____

_____

_____

4. How is the gospel message a story of God showing us mercy? (Romans 3:22-25)

_____

_____

_____

_____

_____

_____

_____

U.S. History and Evangelism

You will be my witnesses.
Acts 1:8 (NIV)

Everyone loves a good story, but for a story to impact us we must find our place in it. Identification with the characters of a story is one thing, but great storytellers help us find our place among the characters. Great storytellers help us enter the story.

For example, I've never really enjoyed European history because it is a lot of work to identify with the people and places within those stories. European history is all about kings and queens and feudal lords, with names that I do not recognize and systems of governance that are strange and confusing. Although I realize that as an American, I have been affected by European history, that my personal experience in this country has been directly impacted by the events that took place in Europe, those connections are hard to make for me. So, when I took European history in college the story always felt impersonal, distant, and disconnected. Simply put, it is hard to find my place in the story of European history.

I am afraid that some of us have experienced salvation this way, impersonal, distant, and disconnected. We know that we have been affected by the events of Jesus' life, death, and resurrection, but at the same time they seem like a distant and foreign reality. Although we may accept that our current existence, as well as our future hope, depends upon those first century events, it can be hard to find our place within the story of salvation.

On the other hand, the subject of U.S. History is very different for me. I love U.S. History, because I can easily identify with the people and places mentioned in the textbooks. U.S. History is all about presidents and first ladies, the birth of a nation and democracy. The names of people and places, as well as the experiences are very familiar to me, so that I not only read the story, but I easily connect with the story. I can quickly see how these former American's lives have impacted my life, not to mention see how my life is impacting other Americans similarly. When I took American history in college it was fun because it was not simply "a" story, it was "my" story and I was able to find my place within the story, as a part of American history unfolding. This is

> *A witness is not someone who has simply read or heard a story, but someone who has found a place within the story.*

how we are to understand our salvation, as well as how we are to read Scripture.

For our sake and for the sake of the world, it is important that we find our place in the story of salvation. It's common for Christians to feel that they would be a better witness for Christ if they would simply acquire certain techniques or skills for sharing their faith. But it's impossible to testify about something we have never really felt a part of. In fact, that's what it means to be a witness.

A witness is someone who has special knowledge. A witness is someone who has experienced something about which they can give firsthand testimony. A witness does not stand outside a story, recounting the characters and events, but a witness is involved in the story and reports their experience of the events. A witness is not someone who has simply read or heard a story, but someone who has found a place within the story.

We must begin reading the Bible not as "the" story of God's work in history, but as God's work of salvation in "our" story. Salvation history is the story of what God has done for you and me. It's a very personal story. The Bible must become our family history, so that Christians are not people with "a" story to tell, but rather people "of" the story. We are not simply called to witness to someone else's life, we are people "of" the story, and that is the offer God is making to all men and women. That is the message we carry to the world, a personal offer to be a part of the unfolding work of God's work in history to save us from our sinfulness.

Going Deeper Questions

1. Do you experience Scripture as "the" story of God's saving work in the world, or as God's work of salvation in "your" story?

   _____

   _____

   _____

   _____

_____

_____

_____

2. To whom are you currently offering a "witness" about Jesus' resurrection?

_____

_____

_____

_____

3. How might your witness be strengthened by seeing the events of Scripture as a part of your own story?

_____

_____

_____

4. What prevents you from more personally finding your place in the story of Scripture?

_____

_____

_____

_____

One New Humanity

His purpose was to create in himself one new humanity
out of the two, thus making peace. Ephesians 2:15 (NIV)

In August 2007, I traveled to Jackson, Mississippi to spend two days with Dr. John Perkins. Born in 1930, in rural Mississippi, Dr. Perkins was the son of sharecroppers. At the age of 27 though, he was born again, which dramatically changed his trajectory in life. The year of his spiritual new birth was 1957 and he immediately began preaching. Throughout the 1960's, John and his wife, Vera Mae, also launched several social welfare programs, aimed at helping the African American community with education and voter registration. During those years, Dr. Perkins marched with Dr. Martin Luther King Jr., and by the fall of 1967 he and Vera Mae were fully immersed in the school desegregation movement. At great personal cost, John even enrolled his oldest son Spencer in the previously all-white local high school.

In the fall of 1969, Dr. Perkins led an economic boycott of the white-owned stores in his hometown. Just six months later, on February 7, 1970 he was arrested and tortured by white police officers, and narrowly escaped lynching. While visiting with Dr. Perkins he drove me by the tree where the officers tied him up and from which they threatened to hang him. Remarkably, he emerged from that near lynching experience with an even greater commitment to gospel ministry. He saw the damage done by racism, in both the white and black communities, and believed that only faith in Jesus would bring healing.

By the mid-seventies, John and Vera Mae were operating thrift stores, health clinics, a housing cooperative, as well as offering classes in Bible and theology in the Jackson area. Together, they successfully integrated the care of souls through gospel preaching and teaching with the care of bodies through ministry to the poor and a call to racial reconciliation. Of course, for these efforts Dr. John Perkins and his wife Dr. Vera Mae Perkins (who is most often referred to simply as "Grandma") have received 13 honorary doctorates from universities all over the nation, and John has served on the board of directors for such distinguished organizations as World Vision and Prison Fellowship.

After landing in Jackson on that hot August morning in 2007, I rented a car and drove to the Perkins Center, which is not far from the downtown. As I approached the property, I saw a man in the front yard wearing bib-overalls and boots. He was firing a rifle into the trees, aiming at what I was not sure. I cautiously pulled into the parking lot, rolled down my window, and asked where Dr. Perkins' office was located. The man in bib-overalls and holding the rifle, took one more shot into the trees, and then directed me to park. He approached my car, still holding the rifle, and introduced himself as Dr. Perkins. Apparently, the noise of the Grackles in the trees was bothering him. Seeing I was speechless, he invited me into his house for lunch.

Vera Mae was in the kitchen. Still in shock to be sitting at John's and Vera Mae's kitchen table, I listened as he waxed eloquent about the God-given role of the church in healing the racial and economic divide within our society. In great detail, John explained how the failings of the Russian Orthodox Church had led to the Bolshevik revolution and the rise of godless Marxism. He leaned across the table and with great conviction asked, "Kelly, do you know what the bishops of the Russian Orthodox Church were doing while Marxists were marching in the streets and leading a revolution?" "No," I mumbled quietly. "The bishops were voting on the color of their robes, oblivious to the suffering of the poor" he said. Then, with the deepest compassion, he said "That's the American church. We are too often worried about how we look, rather than social injustice."

The good news of the gospel is that every nation, tribe, language, and people group are now made one, through faith in Jesus. This means that faith in Jesus is transcultural. All the glories of salvation are reflected in the inclusivity of the gospel. One clear indication of this reality is Bible translation. The Koran, the holy book of Islam, is believed by Muslims to only be "authoritative" when read in Arabic. But the Bible is offered to every culture in their own language, because the message of the gospel is greater than any one culture.

The application is straightforward. God's people will work for economic, social, and racial justice. Although the church does not have a perfect record on matters of justice, particularly here in America. At the same time, it was Christians who led the movement to abolish slavery in both Europe and America, people like John and Vera Mae Perkins who have shown us how to forgive one another and how to bring justice to communities.

Going Deeper Questions

1. What have we historically believed was needed to heal the hostilities and injustices so common within society?

   _____

   _____

   _____

   _____

2. What, if any, racism or bigotry have you experienced?

   _____

   _____

   _____

   _____

3. How have you seen the gospel overcome barriers of race, language and culture?

   _____

   _____

   _____

   _____

4. How does the trans-culturalism of the gospel impact the way we live day to day?

   _____

   _____

   _____

   _____

   _____

Born Again

You should not be surprised at my saying,
'You must be born again.' John 3:7 (NIV)

She had only been attending the church for a couple of months. Yet, I will never forget her asking me bluntly, "Why does everyone keep talking about being born again around here?" When we met to discuss her frustrations, she explained that the words themselves, "born again," had always had a negative connotation for her. Below is a portion of an email I received from her after we met.

> It wasn't until you showed me the passage in the bible, where Jesus tells Nicodemus that he must be born again, that I really did some soul searching and realized that "born again" actually applied to me. It scared me for a while to identify with that statement but I really am a different person now. I don't remember a "moment" that it occurred as everyone seemed to feel that most "born agains" do, but I know that I have been "born again". I can feel and often hear the Holy Spirit in my life.

Jesus did not say that it is simply a good idea, or one option among many, but that we *must* be born again in order to enter the Kingdom of Heaven (John 3:5-7). To be born again means first and foremost to be brought from death to life by God's will.

"Flesh gives birth to flesh," Jesus declared, "but Spirit gives birth to Spirit" (John 3:6). Jesus explained that those who are born again are "born not of natural descent, nor of human decision or a husband's will, but born of God" (John 1:13). This means that we do not cause our new birth. God causes it, which is one of the reasons that the notion of having to be born again makes so many people uncomfortable. The necessity of the new birth clearly outlines our hopeless condition apart from God's intervention. Unless God acts to bring us to life spiritually, we remain dead in our sinfulness (Ephesians 2:1). We like to believe that we can save ourselves, but we cannot cause ourselves to be born again spiritually, any more than we caused ourselves to be born biologically. Being born again is a God thing.

This means that new birth is not simply about getting a new religion, or a new understanding, or new habits. Although, all of these follow from new birth. New birth is about spiritually dead people coming to life through the indwelling Spirit of God. The Apostle Paul describes this event writing "the old has passed away, behold new has come" (2 Corinthians 5:17). To drive the point home, consider the context in which Jesus makes the new birth declaration. Nicodemus came to Jesus at night and said, "Rabbi, we know you are a teacher who has come from God. For no one could perform the miraculous signs you are doing if God were not with him" (John 3:2). In other words, Nicodemus observed the supernatural *in* Jesus. He saw God at work through Jesus' miracles. But, Nicodemus had not experienced the supernatural *of* Jesus—the Spirit's transforming power.

It is interesting to note Jesus' reply to Nicodemus. He doesn't say, "I wish everyone in Palestine could see the truth that you see about me." That's not what Jesus says because he realizes that Nicodemus has not yet experienced new birth. Instead, Jesus says to Nicodemus, "You must be born again," or you will never see the kingdom of God. In other words, what matters is not merely affirming the supernatural *in* Jesus but experiencing the supernatural *of* Jesus. Nicodemus needed to experience the Spirit's new birth.

Again, this can be unsettling. Nicodemus was a Pharisee, which means that he was

> *New birth is not simply about getting new religion, or a new understanding, or new habits. Although, all of these follow from new birth. New birth is about spiritually dead people coming to life through the indwelling Spirit of God.*

highly moral. Do not miss this. Morality does not negate the necessity of the new birth. If humanity was able to earn their way to heaven through moral behavior, then Nicodemus would have been at the head of the line. Truth be told, morality may well make the necessity of new birth all the more obvious in our lives. After all, Nicodemus came to Jesus! This highly religious man still knew that he was lost and in need of something more.

This raises a final issue. Not only is morality insufficient to provide eternal life, so are miracles. Nicodemus had observed Jesus' miracle working power, but observing a miracle was not sufficient to provide him with life. Being amazed by Jesus' brilliant teaching or his power to work miracles saves no one. We are only saved as the Holy Spirit enters our lives and brings us to new life. We are only saved when the Spirit of Jesus miraculously brings us to new life from death.

From our side, we experience new birth as faith in Jesus is awakened in our hearts. Spiritual life and faith in Jesus come into being together. That is to say our new life through the Spirit makes faith in Jesus possible. This means that if you find within yourself a desire to believe that God raised Jesus from the dead, then the Spirit is already at work in your life. Confess with your mouth that Jesus is Lord and Scripture says you will be saved (Roman 10:9).

Going Deeper Questions

1. Why do we experience new birth (John 1:13), and how do we experience new birth, and what is our experience *in* new birth? (1 John 5:4)

   _____

   _____

   _____

   _____

   _____

   _____

_____

_____

_____

_____

2. What do the following passages of Scripture indicate about our experience after new birth?

- 1 John 2:29
- 1 John 3:9
- 1 John 4:7
- 1 John 5:4
- 1 John 5:18

_____

_____

_____

_____

_____

_____

3. How might Ezekiel's description of God's intention to transform his people relate to John's description of our need for new birth? (Ezekiel 36:24-27)

_____

_____

_____

_____

_____

Nicodemus' Journey

The wind blows wherever it pleases. You hear its sound, but you cannot tell where it comes from or where it is going. So it is with everyone born of the Spirit." "How can this be?" Nicodemus asked. John 3:8-9 (NIV)

Nicodemus was a Pharisee, which means that he was wealthy, well educated, and socially powerful. Yet, he went to Jesus under the cover of darkness, and every mention of "darkness" in John's gospel has a spiritual component. In other words, John seems to mention that it's nighttime to give us a sense of the condition of Nicodemus' soul. Like every child in the womb, prior to being born biologically, Nicodemus was in darkness spiritually and he needed to come into the light. He needed to be born, again.

From a human perspective, Nicodemus most likely came at night because he didn't want others to know of his interest in Jesus. Nicodemus was a member of the Jewish Ruling Council, also known as the Sanhedrin, which was a group of 70 men who had jurisdiction (i.e. spiritual authority) over every Jew on earth. Jesus referred to Nicodemus as "Israel's teacher," leading some to believe that Nicodemus may have been considered the resident scholar within the Sanhedrin. In short, Nicodemus was no slouch. He was a diligent student of Scripture, and a devout spiritual leader. But he was also confused and unnerved by what Jesus had to say to him. "How can this be?" Nicodemus asked Jesus. How can someone be born again?

As far as we can tell, these are the last words that Nicodemus ever spoke to Jesus. It's not the last time we read of Nicodemus though in the gospels. In fact, it could be easily argued that John continues to follow the spiritual journey of Nicodemus so that we can watch someone being born again. The second time we read of Nicodemus, he is urging the Sanhedrin to at least hear what Jesus had to say before trying to arrest him. The Jewish Ruling Council would have none of that though, and they shamed Nicodemus into silence (John 7:50).

The final time we hear of Nicodemus, he was working with Joseph of Arimathea to remove Jesus' dead body from the cross and prepare it for burial (John 19). Together, Joseph and Nicodemus took Jesus' lifeless body down from the cross, covered it with 75 lbs. of spices, wrapped it in linen strips and placed it in a tomb. Culturally, we know that this type of care for dead bodies was only carried out by women in the first century and never done by wealthy, well-educated, socially powerful men. The conclusion we are left to draw is that Nicodemus was finally "born again," albeit after a longer gestation period.

Gestation is that period of 40 weeks (280 days), in which a human grows in preparation for physical birth. I suspect that Jesus did not simply adopt the metaphor of new birth, so that we might understand how people come to faith, but rather that God actually *designed* the process of biological birth in order that we might better understand what is required if we are to "see the Kingdom of God." Below is a graph summarizing some of the parallels between biological birth and spiritual new birth.

Much like parents decide to have a child, we know there is a moment in which God decides to save. And just as parents do not consult with their children about whether they want to be conceived, God does not consult with any human about whether they will be elect for salvation. In Ephesians 1:4 we learn that God "chose us in him before the creation of the world."

Biological Birth	Spiritual New Birth
Decision	**Election** – God's decision to save some through new birth (Romans 8:28-29, Ephesians 1:4).
Conception	**Regeneration** – God's act to bring someone from death to new life by his Spirit (John 1:13, John 3:6).
Gestation	**Calling** – Time of spiritual seeking, as one is being drawn by the Father to repentance and public confession of faith in Jesus (John 6:44).
Delivery	**Conversion** – Mankind's physical response to new life by the Spirit through repentance and confession (Romans 10:9-10).

The next spiritual step in the new birth process is regeneration, that moment when someone is brought from death to life by God's Spirit. Just like in conception, there is a singular moment when a sperm fertilizes an egg, causing life to form, similarly there is a moment when spiritually dead people are brought to new life, and it happens apart from anything we do. Jesus said, "Flesh gives birth to flesh, but Spirit gives birth to spirit" (John 3:6), meaning it's not something that humans can control. The Spirit is in charge of this moment. John opens his gospel by writing that those who are children of God are "born not of natural descent, nor of human decision or a husband's will, but born of God. (John 1:13). God causes our new birth (Ephesians 2:4-5).

This means that being born again is not first and foremost about acquiring more knowledge, although having a new understanding is an outcome of new birth. This also means that being born again is not first and foremost about behaving, although living in a completely different way is certainly an outcome of being born again. This is unsettling to some, because it means we are not in control of the process of salvation. We participate in the process, but we do not cause our new birth.

Finally, the last step in the process of spiritual new birth is conversion. This is what we are most often talking about when we urge folks to "make a decision" to trust in Jesus as Savior. Like the physical experience of birth, in which the baby descends the birth canal, the head crowns and they draw their first breath outside the womb, conversion is the first time that a person physically demonstrates, for all the world to see, their new life of faith in Jesus Christ through confession and repentance.

This is most likely what we see in Nicodemus' life when he went with Joseph of Arimathea to care for Jesus' body. This appears to be an act of genuine faith in Jesus. It may not have been his first act of faith, but it certainly appears to be an act by which he was demonstrating the new life he had through faith in Jesus as Savior and Lord (Romans 10:9-10).

Now, between regeneration, which is God's work to bring us to new life by the Spirit, and conversion, which is a human's physical response to the work of God, through repentance and confession, there is the season of "calling." Biologically this parallels gestation, which is that mysterious period of growth, hidden from sight, in which a person is developing in the womb. Spiritually speaking, calling is that mysterious period of spiritual development between darkness and light, as a person is wrestling with when and how they will act in faith. Paul wrote that "those whom he predestined he also called" (Romans 8:30).

Spiritually, this period is often described as a season of "seeking," when folks have strange and unexplained urges to do things like read the Bible, or go to church, or break off a sinful relationship. They begin asking their friends questions of faith, or searching the internet for answers of faith. They often grow tired of their favorite sin and look for ways out of it. This is what was most likely going on in Nicodemus' life as he spoke up on behalf of Jesus in front of the Sanhedrin. While it is certainly true that people may seek answers to spiritual questions who are not being called by God, everyone who is being saved by God will pass through a season of calling, whether short or long.

Now you may be thinking, "Why do I have to do anything if God is the one who is saving me?" Just as a baby does not cause their conception or gestation or delivery, they do at the same time actively participate at each stage. The same is true spiritually. We are involved in the process of our new birth, without causing it. And let's be honest, some babies are born biologically with less difficulty than others, and the same is true spiritually. Some cooperate in the new birth process, and some do not. Some of us were born again through great trauma, and others are born again with relatively little trauma. That's why Scripture says, "do not harden your heart" (Hebrews 13:5).

Going Deeper Questions

1. What was the experience of spiritual "gestation" like for you? If you have not yet been "converted" what are the barriers for you to acting in faith?

_____

_____

_____

_____

_____

_____

_____

_____

_____

_____

2. Based on the testimony of Nicodemus' life, how is the change that Jesus offers different than changes brought by one's effort or knowledge? What place do effort and knowledge have in the Christian life?

_____

_____

_____

_____

_____

_____

_____

_____

_____

3. What do John 1:13, Titus 3:3-7, and 1 John 4:7-8 add to your understanding of "new birth"?

_____

_____

_____

_____

_____

_____

_____

_____

_____

_____

_____

Charismaniacs

*Wearing a linen ephod, David was dancing
before the Lord with all his might. 2 Samuel 6:14*

Early in my tenure as a senior pastor, I visited a staff meeting at another church. It was a much larger church, with six times as many staff. The senior pastor at this church was mentoring me and I was eager to see him lead in his setting. While I certainly learned a lot about effective leadership that day, the lesson that most stands out to me is one on worship.

Toward the end of the staff meeting, after all the formal administrative work was completed, there was a short time of singing together. The church staff numbered about 100, and they all moved to one end of the room and sat around a piano. As the music started, one guy, whom I had not yet met, shot to his feet and thrust both of his arms straight up over his head. My first thought was, "I didn't realize this was a charismatic church!" But then I noticed that no one else stood with him. We sang three or four songs and everyone else remained seated for the entire time of singing.

And it wasn't simply that this guy was standing, alone mind you, or even that his arms were raised that made him so strange. He was also singing very loudly, swaying back and forth, and making motions to the music with his hands in the air. Of course, I was trying hard not to stare. After all, I was supposed to be focusing on God too. But it was like a train wreck. You couldn't help but look.

After worship was over, I immediately asked the senior pastor about the man. He just chuckled. "Yeah," he said, "I probably could have warned you. He can get pretty passionate." The senior pastor went on to explain that this man was once an alcoholic, and that because of his alcoholism he had lost his job, his home, and his family. Then he met Jesus and everything had changed, and he now uses his staff position at the church to help others who are struggling with addiction.

By the end of staff meeting the only person I wanted to talk to, at this very large and highly effective church, was the janitor. His love for God, expressed in passionate praise, made it obvious that he had experienced God's goodness and love at a deep level.

Not unlike that janitor, King David was passionate in his praise of God too. He danced before the Lord, in an "undignified" manor (2 Samuel 6:22). A more contemporary word might be "foolish." What would make someone act publicly "foolish" in their praise of God? The answer is an experience of God's goodness. All that God had promised to do for David, had finally come to pass, and David's response was dancing in public with all his might. What's our response to God's goodness?

In the Gospel of Luke 7:38 we read the story of a woman who is described as sinful. That is to say she was unworthy of God's goodness, just as David was, and just as we are. But she was so deeply impacted by the grace of God that she anointed Jesus' feet with her own tears. You talk about undignified and looking foolish. It was dinner time and Jesus was eating in her village, in the home of a Pharisee, who was a Jewish religious leader in that time.

She entered the home uninvited, interrupted the mealtime conversation, and cried on Jesus' feet. Then she stooped down to wipe his feet with her hair.

Does everyone in the gospels respond this way? No. But time and time again, those who meet with the goodness of God act with total disregard for social and cultural expectations. Zacchaeus, a chief tax collector who was famously short and climbed a tree in order to see Jesus, agreed to pay back four times what he had stolen from the citizens of Israel after he met Jesus (Luke 19:8). And Mary, the sister of Martha, poured a pint of perfume on Jesus' head, the value of which was an entire year's wages (John 12:3-5). How much did you make last year? Can you imagine pouring it out in Jesus' praise?

I would go so far as to say that if no one thinks your expression of love for God is strange, then you might not be enjoying the gospel. You might simply be religious, like Michal was religious, King David's first wife. She condemned David's dancing, saying that he was acting like a fool. Or, you might be religious like the Pharisees were, those with whom Jesus was eating when the sinful woman cried on his feet. The Pharisees condemned Jesus' patience and care for that woman as undignified.

Make sure you understand. I am not saying that we should act foolish and undignified so that God loves us. I am saying that when we catch sight of God's love for us it causes us to do things that will be considered by the culture in which we live as strange. Remember, all our needs have been met in Jesus, and as we experience God's promise keeping care, then our behavior will seem strange in the world.

Going Deeper Questions

1. On a scale of one to ten, how passionate is your public expression of love for God, and why did you give yourself that particular score?

   _____

   _____

   _____

2. Give some contemporary examples of what might be described as "undignified" displays of passion for God? (2 Samuel 6:22)

   _____

   _____

   _____

   _____

3. When have you acted "undignified" in your public expression of love for God?

   _____

   _____

   _____

   _____

4. How have you, or how might you, respond if criticized for a public display of passion for God?

   _____

   _____

   _____

   _____

Fear of Circumstances

Do not be anxious about anything, but in every situation,
by prayer and petition, with thanksgiving present your
requests to God. Philippians 4:6 (NIV)

When my father turned 55, my brother and I celebrated with him by taking a trip to Yellowstone National Park. The trip was great overall, but it was surprisingly cold for August. On our second night camping in the park, the temperature sunk into the 30's, and we spent much of the night huddled in the van cycling the engine on and off to keep warm. About 4:00am we decided to drive around the park looking for wildlife. We figured it would be better than shivering in the van.

As the sun came up a dense fog descended throughout the park, making it difficult to drive and impossible to see any animals, so we pulled off into a little roadside turnout to stretch our legs. The sign at the turnout indicated there was a mile-long boardwalk, and we figured we could walk the boardwalk while the fog cleared. Boardwalks are everywhere in Yellowstone, helping park visitors know exactly where to walk and where not to walk. Hot springs throughout the park are boiling and the ground around the springs can be very soft. The park service provides board walks so there are not as many accidents. No one wants boiled tourists.

We started up the boardwalk, but about a quarter of a mile into the walk we heard a strange sound off in the distance. It was hard to make out. It was clearly an animal of some sort, but we could not see anything because of the fog. We initially figured we were safe as long as we stayed on the boardwalk, but five minutes later, and about a half mile into the walk, the noise started getting louder and it was clearly getting closer. Although unrecognizable, we imagined that the sound resembled the noise that might be made if one were to cross a mountain lion and a bear. My father casually suggested we start jogging back to the van. No more walking.

We had not jogged far when we came upon a portion of the boardwalk that was covered with piles of fresh buffalo dung. We knew it was buffalo dung because we had seen it all over the park in the days prior, and we knew they were fresh because steam was coming off of them. We reasoned that the buffalo must have just come through the area and were probably running from the same noise that we were running from. Not surprisingly our pace quickened. Whatever could scare buffalo was certainly worth avoiding.

By this point, we were in a full sprint, all the while dodging buffalo dung on the boardwalk. Only about a quarter of a mile from the parking lot, the thought of soon finding safety had just passed through my mind when we were forced to an abrupt halt. Because of the fog we could only see about fifteen feet in front of us as we were sprinting down the boardwalk, but the shapes were unmistakable. Buffalo were standing on the boardwalk, two and three deep. I could make out about 10 total in front of us, but there was no telling how many were hidden in the fog. Panicked, the three of us simultaneously turned to run the other way. But there was nowhere to go. There were buffalo behind us as well.

In our effort to escape the terrible noise, we had accidently run right into the middle of the buffalo herd. Thankfully, they were as startled to see us as we were to see them, and there was a priceless moment when we all just stared at each other. It was during that moment of stunned silence, that we realized that the noise from which we were running, was actually the call of the bull in the buffalo herd driving his cows and calves to pasture that morning, and now we were a part of the herd as well.

Of course, we made it out alive. Scared to wander off the board walk because of the hot springs, we squeezed between the buffalo standing on the boardwalk. While this is a fairly humorous example of a fearful circumstance, there are all types of fearful circumstances that are not humorous. What are we to do when the doctor tells us that we have cancer, or our boss tells us that we are fired, or our spouse tells us that they want a divorce? Or, what are we to do when our kids get entangled in addiction? Fear is what we feel when our weaknesses are exposed and it is clear that we are vulnerable to suffering injury and/or loss. How are we to handle our fears?

The Apostle Paul encourages us not to be anxious about anything! Don't be anxious about buffalo, cancer, job loss, divorce, or addiction. Instead present these fearful situations to God in prayer. Is praying all we are to do? No. But it is a primary and essential activity, and it brings God's peace into our lives. Whatever the situation we are facing, God's peace can "guard" us. We need God's peace, because fear can drive us toward making sinful decisions. Fear backs us into the corner, where we are tempted to doubt God's goodness and love for us, from which we make all types of sinful decisions. The real risk in fear is not suffering injury or loss physically, but acting in faithlessness.

Going Deeper Questions

1. How have you historically handled fearful circumstances?

_____

_____

_____

_____

_____

2. What fearful circumstances are you currently facing, and how are you responding?

_____

_____

_____

_____

3. Considering the fearful circumstances that you are currently facing, what requests might you make of God?

_____

_____

_____

_____

Fear of Man

Do not be afraid of those who kill the body but cannot kill the soul. Rather, be afraid of the One who can destroy both soul and body in hell. Matthew 10:28 (NIV)

Long ago, before Sherri and I had any kids, we were getting ready for a date one evening when the phone rang. I answered it downstairs in the kitchen. Sherri was upstairs getting ready. We were in a hurry to leave, as we were late to meet some friends for dinner. It was a telemarketer and I quickly got off the phone and we got out the door.

We stayed out late that night. Again, this was before kids. It must have been after midnight when we finally rolled in, and we headed straight upstairs to bed. Just as we were falling asleep the phone rang again. This was some six hours later mind you, after the earlier call, the one I took just before leaving the house.

Oddly though the phone only rang once. I did not even bother rolling over to reach for the phone beside the bed, because I was so tired. I do remember thinking to myself, "Who would be calling at this late hour?" as I drifted back to sleep. But then I heard a second noise. It was coming from downstairs. Most people would not recognize the sound today, as most homes do not have landlines anymore. But it was a distinct sound for older generations, one that everyone recognized. It was the sound made by a phone left off the receiver. The noise was meant to alert people that the phone was not sitting on its cradle, which meant it would not receive calls.

Foggy, and still half asleep, I sat up in bed and said to Sherri, who was also sitting up by that time, "Does that mean what I think it means?" Remember, the phone had just rung, albeit only once. If the phone was now off the hook downstairs, then it could only mean that someone had taken it off the hook. It was like a scene from a horror movie. We were upstairs in our bed, a handsome young couple roused from sleep by the noise of their downstairs phone off the hook.

Then the noise stopped, which meant either that someone hung it up or that it had "timed out." Again, if you know anything about landlines, then you know that the "off the hook" sound lasted for only one minute. Then it stopped. The silence was deafening, and I reached for the phone next to my bed to see if the landline worked. Nothing. The line was completely dead, which meant that the phone downstairs was still off the hook. So there we were, upstairs, trapped in our own house, with no way to call for help because the phone line was dead. This was long before cell phones, and it was at this point that I turned to Sherri and said, "One of us needs to go downstairs."

Obviously, Sherri and I are OK. There was no one in the house. When I answered the phone earlier in the evening, before we left for our date, I had apparently not hung up the receiver fully. It was a wall-mounted phone, and the receiver must have been only partially balanced on the phone cradle. At midnight, when it rang again, the ringing shook it off the cradle and it fell to the floor, which is where I found the handset when I went downstairs with my baseball bat.

Fear is what we feel when our weaknesses are exposed, and we are vulnerable to suffering injury and/or loss. Of course, not all fear is bad. Some fear is helpful. Our fears can provide the energy needed to stand and fight or run and flee. And while my story is a light-hearted example of a possible intruder in our home, Jesus gave these instructions to his disciples about those who would threaten them.

> Do not be afraid of those who kill the body but cannot kill the soul. Rather, be afraid of the One who can destroy both soul and body in hell. Matthew 10:28 (NIV)

Jesus was warning his disciples that people will attack them because of their faith. His encouragement though was to fear God, not man. Of course, Jesus went on to comfort the disciples as well. "You are worth more than many sparrows" (Matthew 10:31). The message is that God is powerful and to be feared, and that we are precious to him and that he will provide for us.

Again, my story is a lighthearted story. But what about the neighbor who is threatening, or a spouse who is mean, or the kid at school who is aggressive, or the co-workers who are spreading rumors? The real risk in fear is faithlessness. The real risk in fear is that we feel we have no option but to act in a way that dishonors God. In the Psalms we read...

The fear of the LORD is the beginning of wisdom; all those who practice it have a good understanding. Psalm 111:10 (ESV)

It's common today for even Christians to shy away from encouraging a "fear of God." We want to stress that God is loving, but we can't know God's love for us apart from cultivating an appropriate fear of Him. And unfortunately, there are many who have defined the "fear of God" as simply the dreadful expectation of coming judgment. And while it's true that God will judge each of us, that is a shallow definition for the fear of the Lord. The "fear of the Lord" is much more than simply the dread of God's wrath. The fear of the Lord is a reverential awe of God that produces a lifestyle of obedient worship.

To fear God is to recognize our responsibility to him as our Creator. God created the heavens and earth and everything in them and we must accept him as he is and not try to remake him in our own image. An image of the soft, passive and permissive grandfatherly figure is not the Biblical image of God. God has the power to bless us and to judge us, to save us and condemn us, and our experiencing the love of our Creator depends upon our willingness to accept God as God.

So, what are we to do? How do we handle our fears in a constructive and God-honoring fashion? We must face our fears. By facing our fears we can bring them to God, inviting him to address them. The Psalmist wrote, "Even though I walk through the valley of the shadow of death, I will fear no evil for you are with me" (Psalm 23:4).

Going Deeper Questions

1. How have you historically "handled" your fears?

   _____

   _____

   _____

   _____

2. What will focusing on God, rather than your fears, involve moment to moment, day to day? (Romans 12:2)

   _____

   _____

   _____

   _____

3. How have fears that you have faced in the past led you to make decisions of disobedience to God's Word?

   _____

   _____

   _____

   _____

4. Considering Psalm 23, how does it provide both comfort in fearful times, as well as a call to live by faith?

   _____

   _____

   _____

   _____

Hesed

The king asked, "Is there no one still alive from the house of Saul to whom I can show God's kindness?" 2 Samuel 9:3 (NIV)

Mephibosheth was the son Jonathan and the grandson of king Saul. He was a prince, born into privilege, but tragedy struck early in his life when his grandfather and father were both killed on the same day in a battle against the Philistines. To make matters worse, everyone in the king's family ran for their lives, and the nurse of five-year old Mephibosheth accidently dropped him in the chaos. Both of his ankles were broken when he hit the floor (2 Samuel 4:4). Whether the breaks were too complex for ancient medicine to fix, or he simply missed out on the care he needed because of the upheaval in the kingdom, he was never able to walk again. He was permanently crippled and he grew up in exile.

After David became king, he summoned Mephibosheth to the capital city. This summons could have only produced terror in Mephibosheth's heart, as the only possible conclusion for him to draw was that David was looking to solidify his reign by wiping out all possible competitors for the throne. But that's not what happened. Mephibosheth could have never, not in his wildest dreams, predicted what he actually experienced from king David. He was not called in to be put to death. He was called in to be blessed, cared for, shown mercy and receive grace, and all this despite his relationship with former king Saul.

Why this surprising turn of events? Because David had loved Jonathan, Saul's son and Mephibosheth's father, and he wanted to show kindness to Saul's descendants in order to honor Jonathan. In fact, Jonathan and David made a covenant with one another to care for each other's descendants and David was acting toward Mephibosheth in an effort to fulfill that covenant commitment (1 Samuel 20:42).

David's loyalty to keep his commitment, radically transforms the life of Jonathon's son. Mephibosheth is brought out of the city of Lo Debar, which literally means "a place of no pasture," and he was fed from the king's table in Jerusalem for the rest of his life. Mephibosheth was treated just as one of David's sons. It is a beautiful story of kindness, but it is not simply a story between two friends. It is also a picture of the reality for all those trusting in Jesus for salvation. In David's actions toward Mephibosheth we see an example of "God's kindness" shown toward each of us in Jesus Christ (2 Samuel 9:3).

Just as Mephibosheth suffered because he was born into Saul's family, all of humanity suffers because we are born into Adam's family (i.e., the first man). Mephibosheth did not have any say in the family into which he was born. He was born into the family of a king who had acted disobediently and was under God's judgement. As a result, Mephibosheth grew up in exile. We too did not have any say in the family into which we were born. We were each born into Adam's family. As a result, we are each under God's judgement, because of our association with disobedient Adam (Romans 5:12), and we are now living in exile outside of the Garden of Eden.

And just as Mephibosheth was permanently crippled by a fall, humanity is permanently crippled by sin. Mephibosheth was unable to provide for himself. It was not simply that he was exiled. He was also lame, unable to provide for himself. The same is true for us spiritually. We are each unable to provide for ourselves spiritually. It is not simply that we are guilty by association, having inherited our sin state from our spiritual father Adam, we are each unable to provide any remedy for our condition.

The good news though is that what Mephibosheth was unable to do for himself David did for him. More importantly, what humanity was unable to do for ourselves Jesus did for us. Just as king David showed kindness to Mephibosheth, restoring and providing for him from his table, King Jesus has shown kindness to humanity, restoring any who would receive him and providing for them from his table. We have each been summoned by God, and while judgment is what we deserve, loving kindness is what we are offered.

In fact, the Hebrew word translated as "kindness" all three times in this passage is *hesed* (2 Samuel 9: 1, 3, 7) and it is a unique word within the Old Testament. This Hebrew word has a very particular meaning within the Old Testament. While translating *hesed* as "kindness" is appropriate, the word itself has a breadth of meaning that is hard to capture by the English language. No single word in the English language fully captures its meaning. Words like kindness, loving-kindness, steadfast love, mercy, trustworthiness, loyalty, and loyal-love have all been used to translate *hesed*.

This word has a range of meaning in the English language because it is a very particular type of "kindness" that David means to express to Mephibosheth. David wants to show "covenantal" kindness toward Saul's descendants, a kindness fueled not simply by feelings, but a kindness based upon a promise that he had made to Jonathan, Mephibosheth's father. *Hesed* is both affection and selfless loyalty in relationship.

> *Just as king David showed kindness to Mephibosheth, restoring and providing for him from his table, King Jesus has shown kindness to humanity, restoring any who would receive him and providing for them from his table.*

Of the 246 times that *hesed* appears in the Old Testament, the vast majority refer to the vertical relationship people have with God. Biblically, *hesed* is most often understood as the life-giving and life-sustaining kindness of God shown toward humanity, by which we are brought into and kept in relationship with God. This means that when the original author used the word and the original audience heard this word it would have always brought to mind for them God's kindness, steadfast love, and loyalty to his people. There may be no more significant Old Testament description of how God relates to his people than the meaning that this Hebrew word communicates. God loves His people loyally, despite our sinfulness and for our benefit and his glory.

If this grammatical link weren't enough for us to see the story of Mephibosheth as an example of God's mercy shown toward us in Jesus, there is also a clear contextual link. Just two chapters before this story is related, we read these words, which were spoken by the prophet Nathan to David. They are a promise, or a covenant, to David from God about his reign as king.

> Your house and your kingdom will endure forever before me; your throne will be established forever.
> 2 Samuel 7:16 (NIV)

Of course, we know that David died. So how in the world could this promise be fulfilled? What might God have in view when he says that David's throne will be established "forever"? Well look at the words of the angel Gabriel to Mary in describing Jesus.

> The Lord God will give him the throne of his father David, and he will reign over Jacob's descendants forever; his kingdom will never end."
> Luke 1:32-33 (NIV)

Clearly, the Old Testament promises to king David are fulfilled in King Jesus, a King who shows even greater mercy to a much greater number of people.

Going Deeper Questions

1. How would you describe the kindness of God? (Titus 3:4-7)

   _____

   _____

   _____

   _____

2. What effect does experiencing God's kindness have upon our lives? (Romans 2:4, Titus 3:3-8)

   _____

   _____

   _____

   _____

3. When, and from whom, have you experienced God's kindness?

   _____

   _____

   _____

   _____

4. When, and toward whom, have you shown God's kindness?

   _____

   _____

   _____

   _____

Songs of Lament

Be gracious to me, O LORD, for I am languishing; heal me,
O LORD, for my bones are troubled. Psalm 6:2 (ESV)

Country-western song writers might be the secular equivalent of our ancient Psalmists. Here are some of my favorite Country-western song titles.

- I Bought the Shoes that Just Walked Out on Me
- How Come Your Dog Don't Bite Nobody But Me?
- I'm Getting Gray from Being Blue
- The Last Word in Lonesome is Me
- She Got the Goldmine and I Got the Shaft

Psalms is the largest book in the Bible, a collection of 150 songs that were written by several different authors and compiled by the Israelite community over the course of a thousand years. Some of the songs are happy and sing God's praise. Some of the songs offer advice on life and encourage folks to live with wisdom. Some of the songs celebrate the king of Israel and make a call for loyalty to the king and nation. Some of the songs are filled with anger and vengeance and are a plea for justice, as the Israelites faced their enemies. But there is a special category of songs that are dedicated to the emotion of sadness, the Psalms of lament, the country-western songs of the ancient world.

Common themes in lament Psalms are loneliness, rejection, betrayal, disappointment, broken promises, despair, abandonment, death, disease, loss and hurt. These Psalms are characterized by complaining, and questioning God, and often include listing one's problems. For example, the Israelites sang...

> Be gracious to me, O LORD, for I am languishing; heal me, O LORD, for my bones are troubled. I am weary with my moaning; every night I flood my bed with tears; I drench my couch with my weeping. My eye wastes away because of grief; it grows weak because of all my foes. Psalm 6: 2, 6-7 (ESV)

Few of us like to feel sad, and we often do everything we can to avoid the feeling. But sadness is an opportunity to know God better—to experience greater intimacy with God. After all, Psalm 23, the best known of all the Psalms, reminds us that God prepares a table for us "in the presence of our enemies" (Psalm 23:5).

How do we move from avoiding sadness to seeing it as an opportunity to know God's comfort and even his joy?

How do we move from avoiding sadness to seeing it as an opportunity to know God's comfort and even his joy?

Popular culture tells us that if we are sad, then there is something wrong with us. Of course, the truth is that there *is* something wrong with us. Sadness is a result of loss, and we live in a world filled with loss, which is one of the reasons why it is foolish to try and avoid feeling this emotion. Jesus said, "In this world you will have trouble. But take heart! I have overcome the world" (John 16:33).

It's interesting to study the Psalms of lament, because they are filled with both despair and hope. While the Psalms of lament can paint a bleak picture of life, they always also point us ultimately back to the hope we can have when we turn to God and cry out to him. For example, here is the close to Psalm 6.

> Depart from me, all you workers of evil, for the LORD has heard the sound of my weeping. The LORD has heard my plea; the LORD accepts my prayer. Psalm 6:8-9 (ESV)

We can count on redemption because God hears our plea. Country-western songs seldom offer this encouragement, but biblical laments always point us toward the eager expectation of God's certain redemption. It is fine to be sad, even expected. But do not lose hope. You can lose your dog. You can lose your truck. You can even lose your best friend. But count on the certain redemption of God in every situation.

Going Deeper Questions

1. What is your favorite country-western song, and what is your favorite Psalm?

   _____

   _____

   _____

_____

_____

_____

_____

2. On a scale of 1 to 10 how sad are you right now, and what are some of the experiences that contribute to your sadness?

_____

_____

_____

_____

3. Reading Isaiah 61:1-3, why would Jesus use these verses to describe his ministry? (Luke 4:14-21)

_____

_____

_____

_____

4. How have you experienced God's comfort in your mourning?

_____

_____

_____

_____

_____

The Invitation to Wait

*Therefore keep watch, because you do not know
the day or the hour. Matthew 25:13 (NIV)*

When my son, Andrew, was about 14, I purchased
some tickets for us to a Chicago Bull's game. The goal was
some father-son bonding. I purchased the tickets through
a well-known ticket agency, and we were to pick them up
at a window at the United Center.

We rolled up about 30 minutes before the game,
went to the window to get our tickets, but the tickets were
not there. The ticket agency had somehow managed to sell
the same pair of tickets twice, and someone else was
already comfortably sitting in our seats. How can you sell
tickets twice? Apparently, the mistake had something to
do with their online system. The lady behind the glass at
the window said she was sorry, but that we would have to
call the ticket agency and see if they would provide us with
new tickets, or a refund.

Of course, I immediately called the ticket agency
while standing in the atrium of the United Center and
started the long process of trying to navigate their phone
tree, which meant listening to a lot of smooth jazz. Tipoff
was about 20 minutes away at this point. When I finally
got through to a live person, they were apologetic and
offered a refund. I told them that I was standing at the
United Center with my son and did not want a refund. I
wanted to see the game, which led to my listening to more
smooth jazz. Tip off was about ten minutes away at that
point.

Then I remembered that I knew someone with access to the United Center, and while on hold, I borrowed my son's phone and gave my friend a call. So with a phone on both ears, I explained the predicament and asked if he could help. He said he would call me right back, which he did. Five minutes later, we were sitting in an Executive Suite, watching the game, and eating all the Buffalo Wings that our heart desired. Thus, proving the old adage, "it's not what you know in life, it's who you know."

In Matthew 25:1-13, Jesus told a story aimed at describing his second coming. In the parable, Jesus is the bridegroom, and the ten virgins represent the waiting church. The ten virgins were to wait for the bridegroom with their lamps and to lead him into the village, where he would have met his bride. Imagine in your mind's eye a procession under the night sky, the way being lighted by lamps. It would have been beautiful. Unfortunately, five of the virgins were not prepared, because they took no extra oil. They had lamps, but no way to refuel their lamps.

These ancient lamps were fairly simple. They were clay pots that could be held in your hand. You would put oil in the little clay pot and a cloth wick in the oil. The oil would soak the wick, which would burn slowly. But if you were going to be out for a long time, you would need to carry extra oil, so that you could refill your lamp. Having a lamp without oil would be like having a flashlight without batteries. These five young ladies were foolish because if the bridegroom delayed, then they would run out of oil and be unable to celebrate him as they are supposed to do.

Now I know that from a modern perspective, this story seems strange, women sleeping along the roadside for a groom so that they can celebrate his arrival. But the delay of the bridegroom was a standard feature in Jewish weddings of that era. The groom's arrival was often delayed by last minute negotiations between the groom and his new in-laws, negotiations over the terms of marriage. Only when everything was finally agreed upon, would the groom then come to his bride's home,

> *We all want to be judged on our merits, until we realize that we come up short.*

claim her, and bring her in a grand procession to his parent's home for the wedding and reception. Likewise, Christians should be prepared for a delay in Jesus' return.

When the bridegroom did finally arrive, the foolish virgins didn't have enough oil. Unable to do their job, they went back into town to buy more oil and arrived late to the wedding reception. When they arrived the door was shut and they couldn't get into the celebration. They were locked out, much like I had been locked out of the United Center. The bridegroom wouldn't let the foolish virgins in, just like the ticket booth person would not let my son and I into the Bull's game. However, the reason the bridegroom gave to the foolish virgins for not allowing them to enter was, "Truly I tell you, I don't know you" (Matthew 25:12). Again, proving the adage, "it's not what you know, but who you know."

Remember the foolish virgins had lamps, just like the wise had lamps. And the foolish virgins waited on the roadside late into the night, just like the wise had waited. And the foolish woke and trimmed their wicks, just like the wise woke and trimmed their wicks. But the foolish had run out of oil. And when they had run out of oil, they did not have a relationship with the bridegroom, who could open the door for them. Instead, the foolish virgins had something more closely resembling religion. They had diligence and sincere effort, but they did not have a relationship with the bridegroom. And in the end, religious effort will always come up short. At some point, we must stop relying upon ourselves and allow Jesus to provide for us. He's the bridegroom and the doorkeeper of heaven.

That evening at the United Center, I did my best to get in on my own, but I fell short. I ran out of oil so to speak. Admission to the game was outside my control and I couldn't provide for myself. When I found myself without a ticket, I called someone who had access and could get me in. I did not resent the person with whom I had a relationship and through whom I could gain access to the United Center. I didn't get angry that I had to depend upon another person. Instead, I called upon him to help me. That is the gospel. We have a relationship with Jesus, through whom we can gain access into the Kingdom of God. That relationship is built upon trust in his sacrifice on the cross, rather than our religious activities. Christians are those who realize they cannot earn their way into heaven, but that they have a friend who can open the door for them.

Going Deeper Questions

1. What can we say about Jesus' return from these passages? (Matthew 24:42, Matthew 25:6, 2 Peter 3:10)

    _____

    _____

    _____

    _____

    _____

    _____

2. On a scale of one to ten, how would you rate your "readiness" for Christ's return, and why did you give yourself that particular rating? (2 Peter 3:11-12)

    _____

    _____

    _____

    _____

3. How does this parable confirm, or challenge, your understanding of salvation and/or discipleship? (Ephesians 2:8-9)

    _____

    _____

    _____

    _____

    _____

Jars of Clay

We have this treasure in jars of clay to show that this
all-surpassing power is from God and not from us.
2 Corinthians 4:7 (NIV)

Sherri and I spent our 15th wedding anniversary in Door County, Wisconsin. We hiked and biked and took a ferry over to Washington Island, and ate lots of great food. Of course, you cannot go to Door County without doing some shopping, and one of the shops we visited was a pottery shop. Nothing highlights the skill of an artisan quite like working with clay. A skilled craftsman can take what is truly little more than dirt and produce beautiful work of art. Of course, many of the stores in Door County also sell products made of gold and silver, but let's be honest. Any craftsman working with gold or silver has a leg up on those working with clay. When a piece of pottery catches our eye, it is because we ae stunned by the skill of the craftsman, not the materials with which they are working! No one is struck by the beauty of clay, until it is shaped, glazed and fired under intense heat, painted and polished. In a similar respect, we are jars of clay, meant to display the power of God, who is the artist of our souls.

While it is true that some feel more like vessels of gold or silver, rather than earthen vessels, we are still just jars of clay. We may be tremendously successful, but we are still just jars of clay, which is not to say that we are worthless. The truth is we are of immense value. God himself died on a cross to redeem us. But our righteousness, when compared with God's, is like dirt.

We all want to experience the "all-surpassing power" of God, but for that to happen we must come to terms with what it means to carry the "treasure," which is Jesus, as fragile and flawed people. We must come to terms with our weaknesses and our failures, and learn to celebrate the treasure who is Jesus. God wants to display his power in our marriages and in our families and in our careers, despite our earthen qualities, our flaws and foolishness, if we will only admit we are simply clay pots. If we will only lay aside arrogance and embrace the humility appropriate for earthen vessels, we will experience the power of God.

Where do we show arrogance? Consider how many parents are willing to pay top dollar for their kids to have tutors, not to mention pay big bucks for their children to have various private music lessons. However, those same parents many times refuse to go to individual or marital counseling. Are we not just clay pots? For some reason we clearly see the need for our children to have the best coaches and tutors available, but when it comes to getting help for ourselves, too many feel as though they are supposed to have all the answers.

We will also hire all types of specialists to help us with the external matters of life, but we resist admitting that we do not have all the answers to the internal issues of life. Who cares about the landscaping and the drapes and the furniture and the 401K, the external matters of life, if on the interior we are losing our soul? As jars of clay we must learn to live at peace with our weaknesses, allowing God to work on our broken lives.

Of course, being at peace does not mean that we do not care that we are weak. Being at peace means that we are confident that God can work in and through us despite our weaknesses. It means that we are confident that God can demonstrate his all-surpassing power in our lives, despite our struggles.

We know that we are living at peace with our identity as clay pots when we act to address our weaknesses rather than avoid or deny them. Avoiding or denying our weaknesses is to hold God at arms-length and it prevents him from working in our lives. We are living at peace with our weaknesses when as alcoholics we attend our AA meetings faithfully, and when as compulsive shoppers we live on a budget, and when as power hungry executives we resist posturing in the boardroom.

So much in my life can be explained by natural human ability or by hard work, but Paul says he intentionally "preached not with wise and persuasive words" (1 Corinthians 2:4) so that the Spirit's power could be clearly seen, so that his ministry could rest on the supernatural work of God. In other words, Paul took intentional steps to depend upon the Spirit's power. What steps are we taking in life so that our "faith might not rest on men's wisdom, but on God's power"?

Maybe taking a step of faith will mean going to counseling and allowing a godly person with wisdom to coach you in your areas of weakness. Maybe a step of faith will mean confessing to your spouse an area of failure. If you are a student, then engage your teacher in a spiritual conversation, or bring Jesus up at the lunchroom table. God longs to demonstrate his power through us, but we must place ourselves in positions that require a demonstration of the Spirit's power. I can tell when I am probably missing out on the Spirit's power in my life, because I am not taking risks. Instead, I work to avoid situations that might make my earthen qualities too obvious, not wanting my imperfections to be seen by others.

Going Deeper Questions

1. What weaknesses are you tempted to deny, pretending that they do not exist?

   _____

   _____

   _____

   _____

2. When have you experienced God's all-surpassing power at work in you?

   _____

   _____

   _____

   _____

3. What steps of faith might you take to experience more of God's all-surpassing power?

   _____

   _____

   _____

   _____

Immanuel

Therefore, the Lord himself will give you a sign:
The virgin will conceive and give birth to a son,
and will call him Immanuel. Isaiah 7:14 (NIV)

During the prophet Isaiah's ministry, the Promised Land was divided into two nations. There was the Northern kingdom, named Israel, and the Southern Kingdom, named Judah. Israel and Judah had long enjoyed a season of peace, but Tiglath-pileser III, had come to power in Assyria, and was pushing southwest, looking to expand his kingdom. All the nations of the area were scrambling to defend themselves.

Israel, the Northern Kingdom, made an alliance with Aram, a neighboring nation on her northern border. Together, they believed that they would be able to turn back an Assyrian invasion. The problem for Judah was that once Israel and Aram cemented their alliance, they launched an attack against Jerusalem, Judah's capital. Their goal was to use Jerusalem's resources to defend themselves against Assyrian attack. This of course sent Judah's king Ahaz reeling, because he did not feel that Jerusalem could withstand an attack. But God sent Isaiah to comfort and guide Ahaz. Isaiah said to Ahaz:

> Be careful, keep calm and don't be afraid. Do not lose heart because of these two smoldering stubs of firewood—because of the fierce anger of Rezin and Aram and of the son of Remaliah. Isaiah 7:4 (NIV)

Ahaz had a decision to make. He needed to decide whether he believed God was able to save his kingdom. You can imagine how hard trusting God would have been for Ahaz. His capital city was surrounded by enemy forces, but Isaiah said to trust in God. It sounds almost as difficult as believing in the salvation provided by a baby, who was born in a stable. Humanity is surrounded by sin, but the gospel says trust in Jesus, the little baby "asleep in the hay" for deliverance.

Unfortunately, Ahaz did not trust in God, and he turned to Assyria for help. In a politically astute but spiritually faithless move, Ahaz created an alliance with Tiglath-pileser III, saying: "I am your servant. Come up and rescue me from the attacking armies of Aram and Israel" (2 Kings 16:7-9). Then he took the silver and gold from the Temple in Jerusalem and he sent it as a gift to the Assyrian king in order to buy his protection. It was apparently more comfortable for Ahaz to rely upon his political expertise than to rely upon God.

Do you see our modern Christmas parallel? God has provided a way for humanity to escape death through faith in Jesus' miraculous birth, and we must decide whether we will trust in God or ourselves. God saw that Ahaz needed help in believing in the deliverance he would provide because he offered him a sign.

> Again the LORD spoke to Ahaz, "Ask the LORD your God for a sign, whether in the deepest depths or in the highest heights." But Ahaz said, "I will not ask; I will not put the LORD to the test." Isaiah 7:10-12 (NIV)

God was willing to provide any sign that Ahaz wanted, but he would have none of it. It's at this point that some believe Ahaz even offered his son in pagan sacrifice to Assyria's gods (2 Kings 16). Since Assyria was Ahaz's hope for deliverance, it is possible he felt he needed their approval through sacrifice. It's against this backdrop that Isaiah offers his famous birth announcement, the sign of God's promise to deliver.

> Then Isaiah said, "Hear now, you house of David! Is it not enough to try the patience of humans? Will you try the patience of my God also? Therefore, the Lord himself will give you a sign: The virgin will conceive and give birth to a son, and will call him Immanuel. Isaiah 7:13-14 (NIV)

While this prophecy is offered in the presence of Ahaz, it's meant for all of humanity. God offered the promise of his deliverance from sin, 700 years before Jesus' birth in Bethlehem. Remember Isaiah's warning to Ahaz? "Be careful, keep calm and don't be afraid. Do not lose heart…" (Isaiah 7:4) Of course, Ahaz was careless with his family, offering his son in sacrifice. He was careless with his kingdom, vowing servitude to Assyria. And, he was careless with his wealth, paying homage to Assyria. What careless decisions are we considering, because we are losing heart? To act with faith, rather than fear, we will need to look at the promises in God's Word rather than the circumstances that are difficult.

Going Deeper Questions

1. What about King Ahaz's refusal to trust in God did you find discouraging and/or challenging? (Isaiah 7:1-17 and 2 Kings 16)

    _____

    _____

    _____

    _____

2. What circumstances are threatening you currently?

    _____

    _____

    _____

    _____

3. What activities would increase your sense of calm, so that you don't act carelessly?

    _____

    _____

    _____

    _____

4. Where can you take bold steps in the days ahead in order to demonstrate trust and hope in God's promises?

    _____

    _____

    _____

    _____

Wisdom

I am the light of the world. If you follow me, you won't be stumbling through the darkness, because you will have the light that leads to life." John 8:12 (NIV)

Some of the wisest people I have known are the parents of my best friend in high school. Sam and I met our freshman year and I spent lots of time in his home. Although wise, Sam's parents are not people whom you would pick out of a crowd. They dress plainly, and they are quiet, even a little awkward socially. They aren't wealthy either. In fact, they lived in a small three-bedroom ranch that was poorly decorated, and they drove old cars.

As a teenager, I remember the wallpaper in the living room of Sam's house was coming off the walls. In fact, for the entirety of my high school experience the wallpaper rolled slowly down the wall. I took my wife to meet Sam's parents 15 years after graduating from high school and the house looked exactly the same. Nothing had changed. But their clothes and cars, social mobility and decorating notwithstanding, the wisdom of Sam's parents is easy to see.

For example, Sam's parents raised five children in that little three-bedroom ranch, and they put all five of their kids through private colleges, as well as a couple of them through seminary, without ever taking out any loans and all on a single income. Sam's mom was a homemaker and Sam's dad was a welder. Sam's mom was joyful and kind and Sam's father was tireless. Sam's parents have been married 63 years.

A few years ago, Sam sent me a newspaper clipping from an article that had been written about him. Sam's a pastor and he was starting a new church. It was the goal of the reporter to help introduce Sam and his new church to the area. When the reporter asked him, "Who is your greatest living hero?" Sam named his

> *All religions agree that humanity is plagued by selfish attitudes and actions. They differ on the remedy.*

father. All of Sam's four other siblings are followers of Jesus, and all of them are serving in their local church. Sam's parents served diligently themselves in the local church. In fact, they attend two churches in their hometown, both of which they helped start. How can we live with such wisdom?

All religions agree that humanity is plagued by selfish attitudes and actions. They differ on the remedy. Buddhism, Hinduism, Islam and Humanism all teach that through various combinations of education and discipline mankind can escape the darkness brought by selfishness. All evidence is to the contrary though. The truth is that more people have access to more education than ever before, but darkness in the world is increasing.

Education falls short of providing a remedy for human selfishness because it simply orders life in a dark world, much like a blind person orders the furniture in their home so that they don't bump into it. Discipline also falls short, because it only addresses the fruit of the problem, and never gets to the root, the seat of our dark desires. While we may gain greater will-power over a particular habit, our desires remain unchanged.

What we need is to address the darkness in our hearts, the ugly attitudes of selfishness and pride that bring destruction into our lives. And that's exactly how Jesus described himself, as "the light of the world" (John 8:12). Christianity's remedy is unlike all other religions. Christianity isn't suggesting greater education or discipline as the cure. Christianity is offering the Light, a person, Jesus, as the cure. His presence enters our lives and chases away the darkness of selfishness and pride.

I sat with a man who had just accepted Jesus into his life and he described a change in his longings—no more wanting to lie or cheat or take revenge on those who had hurt him. His desires had actually changed. For the first time in his life, he wanted to live in the light, and he had the power needed to do so. It is true that Jesus was a brilliant teacher. He taught us to...

- Do to others as you would have them do to you.
- Forgive, just as we need to be forgiven by God.
- Turn the other cheek, to those who harm you.
- Pray for those who persecute you.

While it is true that Jesus was a brilliant teacher, it is a mistake to think that Jesus is only offering us insight and calling us to greater discipline. Sam's parents were followers of Jesus. Jesus had changed their sinful desires by shining his life-giving light into their darkened hearts.

Rather than cultivating selfish attitudes and activities, they lived simple lives of service and generosity to family and community, putting others first, just as Jesus taught them to do. We access the life changing light of Jesus Christ by faith in his miraculous birth, sacrificial death and powerful resurrection.

Going Deeper Questions

1. Whom do you know who lives a life of wisdom, and what about their life stands out to you?

   _____

   _____

   _____

   _____

2. What substitutes for Jesus' light do people offer in answer to the troubles in this world?

   _____

   _____

   _____

   _____

3. How have you experienced the light of Jesus?

   _____

   _____

   _____

   _____

An Organism

In Christ we, though many, form one body, and each member
belongs to all the others. Romans 12:5 (NIV)

One of the largest living organisms in the world is a grove of Aspen trees. It's called a "clonal colony," which means that the grove is one living organism that sends up multiple "stems." The individual stems, or trees, share a common root system. As the trees grow to maturity, they eventually age, die and fall over, but the organism lives on. One of the largest known colonies is a forest of Aspens in Colorado, covering 106 acres. This grove has about 40,000 trees, and is thought to be 80,000 years old. Yet, this grove of Aspens has nothing on the body of Christ. While biologists would not recognize those who are in Christ as one living organism, we are exactly that. Christians are one body, each belonging to one another.

Too often we think of the church as an organization. But the Church is better described as an organism, a living breathing, growing and multiplying community. Like the clonal colony of Aspen trees, Christians share the same root system. We are connected by our common faith in the person and work of Jesus, and as a consequence share in the same Holy Spirit.

Thinking of yourself as "in" Christ has staggering implications! First, we realize that we are no longer alone! Sin, with which we are all born, disconnects us from God and one another. But through faith in Christ we are joined to God, as well as to one another (2 Corinthians 5:18). We may have lots of connections in this world and still be alone. In fact, the connections that men have while sitting at a bar sipping beer, or that athletes have playing on team together, or that family members share in their living room is only a shadow, or a hint, of the connection that God intended for us to experience. While there are certainly deep connections with friends and family members in this world, the deepest connection is only provided when the barrier of sin, which separates us from God and one another, is addressed. Spiritual and eternal connection comes only through trusting in Jesus' death for the forgiveness of sin.

In 2012, the April 2nd edition of Newsweek magazine ran a cover story titled "Forget the Church and Just Follow Jesus." Andrew Sullivan wrote the article and the title provided a pretty good summary of the article's content. Sullivan argues that the Church has been destroyed by politics, poor pastoral leadership and greedy evangelists, and he urges Christians to exit the Church and to simply follow Jesus. I do not disagree with much of the emotion in Sullivan's article. In fact, I wrestle with disappointments from my Church experience too, and in my role as pastor I am sure that I have added to the disappointments of others. But, according to Paul, leaving the Church because it has problems would be like cutting off your nose because you have a cold. We must realize that we implicate ourselves when we criticize the Church, because we are members of the one body. G.K Chesterton, a twentieth century British journalist and respected Christian apologist, was famously asked, "Mr. Chesterton, what is wrong with the world?" To which he responded, "I am!"

The Church is a gathering not of perfect people, but forgiven people. That means there is going to be difficulty and disappointment and discouragement within the Church. At the same time, participation in the Church is not optional. The theologian Augustine put it well when he said; "He cannot have God for his Father who does not have the Church for his mother." Participation in the Church is not optional. We cannot choose to separate from the Church, any more than our right arm can choose to separate from our torso.

Being "in" the body also means we are freed from competition. So many relationships in life are positioned as "win/lose" experiences, but the "win/lose" dichotomy does not apply to relationships within the body of Christ. What is good for one member of the body is good for all. And what is bad for one member of the Church is bad for all. The question is no longer, "What is best for me?" but rather, "What is best for us?"

Going Deeper Questions

1. Besides a "body," what other metaphor can you think of to describe the Church?

   _____

   _____

   _____

   _____

   _____

   _____

   _____

2. Considering the following passages of Scripture below, how else is the church described? (Galatians 6:10, Romans 12:5, Ephesians 2:19-22, Revelation 19:7)

_____

_____

_____

_____

_____

3. Why are some people's connections to the Church weakened and how are some people's connection to the Church strengthened?

_____

_____

_____

_____

_____

4. How would you describe your current connection to the people of God (e.g., fragile, weak, growing, strong), and how could it be strengthened?

_____

_____

_____

_____

_____

The Wind of God

So it is with everyone born
of the Spirit. John 3:8 (NIV)

Picture in your mind's eye several thin and brightly colored ribbons, like the ones you might use to decorate the wrapping of a birthday present. Now imagine these ribbons, not tied to a birthday present, but tied to the front of a fan, with the ribbons blowing as the fan blades spin. As you picture the ribbons blowing, here's my question. What makes the ribbons move?

Maybe you'd answer that the fan blades are making the ribbons move. And the fan blades spinning is an obvious part of the ribbon's movement. But another person could just as accurately say that electricity is turning the fan blades and making the ribbons move. Truth is that both would be right to an extent. The fan blades and electricity both play a part in the ribbon's movement.

The problem is that neither the electricity nor the fan blades are touching the ribbons. The ribbons are moving, but only indirectly because of the fan blades and the electricity. Instead, there is a third agent who touches the ribbons. This unseen agent is powerful, albeit invisible and mysterious, but it would be most accurate to say that wind is moving the ribbons.

It's true that electricity is powering the fan and turning the blades, which are stirring the wind. But only the wind touches the ribbons, causing them to move. While we can't see the wind, we know it is there. We don't know where the wind came from or where it is going after it touches the ribbons, but we know when it's present because of its effect upon the ribbons.

Much like electricity, God the Father is the source of power behind the scenes. And much like the fan, the Son of God has a visible role in redemption. His life and death and resurrection were readily available for all to see, as the Son came in the flesh and gave his life on the cross. But the Spirit is the invisible agent, powerful but mysterious. Like the wind we can't see him, but we know he is there, because we see his effect on our lives. We don't know where he came from or where he is going, or all that he is doing, but we know when he is present, because we are moved. Jesus said:

> The wind blows wherever it pleases. You hear its sound, but you cannot tell where it comes from or where it is going. So it is with everyone born of the Spirit. John 3:8 (NIV)

The spiritual rebirth process takes place as the Holy Spirit blows into our lives. Although we can't see him, or the powers that move him, we can see the effect he has upon us, bringing us to new life through faith in the Son of God. What's the effect of the Holy Spirit in our lives? When the Holy Spirit blows into our lives we are convicted. Speaking of the Holy Spirit, Jesus said:

> When he comes, he will convict the world concerning sin and righteousness and judgment: concerning sin, because they do not believe in me;

249

concerning righteousness, because I go to the Father, and you will see me no longer; concerning judgment, because the ruler of this world is judged. John 16:8-11 (ESV)

The word "convict" is best understood from a legal perspective. Much like a jury would be persuaded to believe the facts in a case by an attorney. In short, the Holy Spirit is the person who convinces people of their need to trust in Jesus, and cares for all those who are trusting in Jesus.

It's ironic that the most common excuse among Christians for not sharing their faith is that we don't know what to say. How many times have we backed away from an opportunity to speak up, whether about sin, or about Jesus' righteousness or about the coming

> *It's the Spirit's job to convince people. Our job is simply to convey the message.*

judgement, because we don't feel that we can convince someone. Surprisingly though, the truth is that we cannot convince anyone that they are sinful, or that Jesus is the Son of God, or that judgment is coming. Only the Holy Spirit can convict someone, which is not to say that there is no need to try and explain the Scripture to people. Matter of fact, the Holy Spirit uses people to communicate the truths of Scripture to others. But communicating the truths of Scripture is not the same as convicting someone of their truthfulness. The move from doubting to believing is always a supernatural work as the Holy Spirit moves in the minds and hearts of people to cause them to believe. It's the Spirit's job to convince people. Our job is simply to convey the message. We don't have to be eloquent, just faithful.

Going Deeper Questions

1. When and how have you experienced the Holy Spirit's convincing work in your life? (1 Corinthians 2:14)

   _____

   _____

   _____

   _____

2. What does John 16:1-15 say about the relationship between the Holy Spirit and humanity?

   _____

   _____

   _____

   _____

3. What are one or two ways you would like to increase your dependence on the Holy Spirit?

   _____

   _____

   _____

   _____

Unity

Make my joy complete by being like-minded, having the same love, being one in spirit and of one mind. Philippians 2:2 (NIV)

It's easy to think that being "like-minded" is a call to agreement. It's not. It's a call to unity, which is different and far better. For example, in Acts 15, Luke records that Paul and Barnabas were getting ready for their second missionary journey when they had a "sharp" disagreement about whether to invite John Mark on the trip (Acts 15:39-40). John Mark had deserted Paul and Barnabas during their first missionary journey and Paul did not think it wise to include him again. Luke doesn't indicate why John Mark deserted them, but simply that Barnabas was willing to take him along a second time. Luke wrote:

> They had such a sharp disagreement that they parted company. Barnabas took Mark and sailed for Cyprus, but Paul chose Silas and left, commended by the brothers to the grace of the Lord. Acts 15:39-40 (NIV)

What are we to make of this? We have two spiritually mature men disagreeing over how to proceed in ministry. And not just any disagreement. It was a "sharp disagreement," which brought their ministry partnership to an end, at least for a while. Did this mean that they were no longer unified? Did this mean Paul and Barnabas were not like-minded? Did this mean that they, whether one or both, needed to repent of sin? No!

It's true that agreement is better than disagreement, but being "one in spirit and mind" has nothing to do with whether to include John Mark. Being "one in spirit and mind" means focusing together on bringing glory to the Son of God, and there are thousands of different ways to accomplish that goal. For Barnabas it meant including John Mark, but for Paul it meant partnering with Silas.

Disagreement doesn't always indicate disunity. It can, but it doesn't have to. We can be "like-minded," "having the same love," and "being one in spirit and mind," and still not agree on a particular matter. When we mistake disagreement for disunity, we are tempted to bow to the idol of uniformity. Unity is not uniformity. I know a church in California that offers 20 different weekend worship services, one of which features country western music and another service features grunge. The unity provided by faith in Christ is not so weak that these types of disagreements should disrupt our connection to God or one another.

Unfortunately, some point to the many denominations within Christianity and claim that unity doesn't exist. We often, and wrongly, assume that having different denominations indicates that there is little doctrinal agreement among Christians. That is not the case. In fact, denominations were originally formed to preserve the unity among Christians, while allowing for disagreement over certain "non-essentials." For example, some have wanted the freedom to celebrate communion on a particular day or with a particular frequency, or to baptize in a certain way, believing that the Bible prescribed a particular form for these practices. Denominationalism allows for a distinction to be drawn between what is a passionate theological conviction (e.g., mode of baptism), and what is a vital theological conviction (e.g., deity of Jesus Christ). Denominations allow for important differences of opinion, while preserving unity on essentials (i.e., anything pertaining directly to salvation).

In this way, the Church is not dissimilar to an egg, having unique strength by design, while at the same time requiring tender care. We all know that eggs are fragile, and for that reason we don't play catch with them. At the same time, few realize how strong is the design of an egg. Did you know that eggs are designed to withstand tremendous force end to end? You can't break an egg by pressing on its poles. This is how hens can sit on eggs and they don't crack, and this is why eggs are packaged and safely shipped vertically, rather than horizontally.

Try this little test at home. Take an egg. Hold it over the sink and press as hard as you can on the two ends. It will not break. Be careful not to touch the side of the egg though while you are pressing on the two ends, because that will make quite a mess.

Our relationships within the Church are much like the design of an egg. Our relationships are fragile, and need to be handled delicately, with tenderness and compassion. At the same time, our unity through faith in Christ is not weak. The Church is built upon the confession that we are saved by God's grace through faith in the death and resurrection of Jesus, apart from anything we do (Ephesians 2:8-9). That confession has withstood immense pressure over the last two thousand years.

Going Deeper Questions

1. Why is the unity provided through faith in Jesus unique? (Acts 4:12, 1 Corinthians 12:12-13, Philippians 2:1, Colossians 1:15-23)

   _____

   _____

   _____

   _____

   _____

   _____

   _____

   _____

2. How would you describe the "marks" of unity outlined in Philippians 2:1-2?
   o Being like minded (Romans 8:5-8)
   o Having the same love (1 John 3:14)
   o Being one in spirit and purpose (Colossians 3:12-14)

   _____

   _____

   _____

   _____

   _____

   _____

   _____

   _____

3. How is the unity provided through Jesus both strong and fragile?

_____

_____

_____

_____

_____

_____

_____

_____

_____

4. When/how have you seen disagreements between Christians mistaken for disunity?

_____

_____

_____

_____

_____

_____

_____

_____

_____

_____

_____

_____

_____

Promptings

Do not quench the Spirit. Do not treat prophecies with contempt but test them all; hold on to what is good, reject every kind of evil.
1 Thessalonians 5:19-20 (NIV)

In January of 2013, I had a dream, a prompting from the Holy Spirit. In the dream, my family was walking together in the woods. Picture something along the lines of a nature walk, nothing too strenuous. It was pleasant. We were enjoying one another and the surroundings. When, out of nowhere, a tornado descended, picked up my son, Andrew, and carried him off away from the family. During the dream, even while it was unfolding, I began to pray for Andrew, crying out to God for his rescue.

In the next scene of the dream, I saw Andrew as he was set down by the tornado and then he rejoined the family on the nature walk. I remember during the dream, feeling thankful and comforted that he was returned to us. At the same time, I woke from the dream feeling concerned, not knowing what it all meant. Lying awake in my bed after the dream, I prayed some more and then faded back off to sleep. The next morning, I shared the dream with Sherri and we both felt comforted as well as concerned, and we resolved to continue to pray.

About three weeks later, a mother of one of Andrew's friends called Sherri to report that she had caught her son, along with Andrew and another one of their friends, doing something that was very dangerous. Later that day I confronted Andrew. He admitted his participation, and we took the actions that we thought best to help him separate himself from those particular behaviors. It was a scary time for us as parents, but I remembered the dream that I had and was comforted to think that God would rescue Andrew from this tornado. I was also moved to pray, prompted very specifically to ask for Andrew's freedom and rescue.

A prompting is a stirring of the Holy Spirit given to move us according to God's plans and for God's purposes. A prompting might include a dream. Of course, not every dream we have is a prompting from the Holy Spirit. Most of the dreams I have are because I ate too much before bed, but the Lord does use dreams to stir his people to action. A prompting might also include a vision that inspires. The Apostle Peter had a vision that led him to travel to Caesarea and share the Gospel with folks he would have otherwise never met (Acts 10). A prompting might include a prophecy (i.e., a divine message) that challenges us, moving us to begin a new discipline, or stop a particular sinful habit, or even undertake a new ministry. Timothy received a prophecy about the role he was to play in the early church (1 Timothy 1:18).

> *A prompting is a stirring of the Holy Spirit given to move us according to God's plans and for God's purposes.*

Of course, dreams, visions and prophecies are not the only possible promptings that the Holy Spirit uses to move us. These are simply the ones that Peter referenced on the day of Pentecost (Acts 2:1-13). There are all types of gifts given to followers of Christ, which the Holy Spirit prompts us to use for the benefit of others and God's glory (Romans 12:6-8, 1 Corinthians 12:8-10, Ephesians 4:11, 1 Peter 4:8-11).

For this reason, believers are warned not to quench (i.e. put out) the promptings of the Holy Spirit (1 Thessalonians 5:19). Just like one might put out a fire with a giant bucket of water, we are to be careful not to pour water on the fire of the Spirit. The Holy Spirit wants the heat of his influence turned up in our lives, and we control the thermostat. Paul in fact, told Timothy to "fan into flame" the gifts he had received from the Holy Spirit (2 Timothy 1:6). It's not that we control the Spirit. But we do control our attitudes and our actions, which are either in step with the Sprit or out of step with the Spirit (Galatians 5:25). Because the Spirit is God, he has a will and a purpose and a role within redemptive history. He is on the move. He is saving the lost, restoring relationship, healing the broken and setting captives free from sinful entanglements. At any given moment we are either opening or closing ourselves to the Spirit's work by how we respond to his promptings.

Going Deeper Questions

1. Have you ever had a dream or vision that you wondered if it was from the Holy Spirit? How did you respond to the dream or vision?

    _____

    _____

    _____

    _____

2. How have you most typically experienced God's promptings in the past?

    _____

    _____

    _____

    _____

3. How have you seen your gifts used by God to prompt others to action?

    _____

    _____

    _____

    _____

4. What steps might you take to experience more of God's promptings in the future (Romans 12:2)?

    _____

    _____

    _____

    _____

Falling Asleep

The mind governed by the flesh is death, but the mind governed by the Spirit is life and peace. Romans 8:5-6 (NIV)

When our children were elementary age they would often make their way into our bedroom in the middle of the night, complaining that they couldn't fall asleep. They would do this despite a long and involved bed-time ritual that included reading, singing, and praying together, activities all of which were aimed at getting them to wind down, in hopes that sleep would come.

Alas, it was inevitable that one of them would come bouncing down the hall not soon after we had turned out the lights saying: "Daddy, I just can't sleep!" In the most loving and compassionate voice I could muster (bear in mind that this was after a 40-minute bedtime ritual), I'd say, "Honey, that's because you are standing beside my bed. You need to be lying down with your eyes closed, if you are going to fall asleep." And I would lead him or her back to bed.

Experiencing the work of the Holy Spirit in our lives is a lot like trying to fall asleep. Just as our bodies naturally long for sleep, Christians long for more of the work of the Holy Spirit in their lives. But we can't make ourselves fall asleep, any more than we can force the Holy Spirit to work in our lives. But we can open ourselves to His work by making sure our mind and body aren't in the way, by making sure we don't present any physical barriers to His work in our lives.

Although we can't make ourselves fall asleep, we can help the process by getting in a dark room, lying down on a soft mattress, turning out the lights and thinking about soothing things. In a similar vein, Paul encourages us to make sure our bodies aren't a barrier to the Spirit's work in our lives. He wrote:

> The mind governed by the flesh is death, but the mind governed by the Spirit is life and peace. Romans 8:5-6 (NIV)

All Christians have the Holy Spirit dwelling within them. The issue is whether we are submitted to the Holy Spirit's control. In each decision we stand at an intersection and must choose who to follow, the flesh, which calls us away from God's plans and purposes for our lives, or the Spirit. Are our minds governed by the Spirit? Do we even know what the Spirit desires? Below is a small comparison of the differences between the desires of the flesh and the Spirit.

Flesh	Spirit
Control	Faith (Hebrews 11:6)
To be served	To serve others (Matthew 20:28)
Wealth	Generosity (2 Corinthians 8:2)
Exaltation	Humility (Philippians 2:2)
Vindication	Justice & Mercy (Micah 6:8)
Sensuality	Purity (1 Corinthians 6:19-20)

To make this a reality, we must tirelessly guard our minds, paying close attention to what preoccupies our thoughts during the day. What concerns engross us? What are we focused on, concentrating on, daydreaming about? So many long to hear and respond to the Spirit's leading, but our minds are filled with thoughts that prevent us from hearing the Spirit's voice.

Most simply put, we will become what we think about. If our minds are filled with thoughts of doubt, lust, greed, worry, fear, anger, then those thoughts will guide our behavior. But if our minds are governed by what the Spirit desires then the Spirit is able to guide our actions. Our minds are the gateway to the experiences of our lives.

In fact, Paul moves from considering the habits of our minds to addressing the actions of our bodies, encouraging us next to consider how we are using our bodies.

> Therefore, brothers and sisters, we have an obligation—but it is not to the flesh, to live according to it. For if you live according to the flesh, you will die; but if by the Spirit you put to death the misdeeds of the body, you will live. Romans 8:12-13 (NIV)

If we are frustrated with not being able to understand God's direction and prompting through the Holy Spirit, then an important element to consider is how you are using your body. What comes out of your mouth? What do your hands touch? What do your eyes look at? Where do your feet go? What do you listen to?

Going Deeper Questions

1. Compare Romans 8:1-17 to Galatians 5:13-25. What appears to be similar between the two passages and what seems to be different?

    _____

    _____

    _____

    _____

2. What do the above passages offer as help to you in saying "Yes" to the Spirit?

    _____

    _____

    _____

    _____

3. Describe a time you've said "No" to the flesh?

    _____

    _____

    _____

    _____

4. If you began to say "Yes" to the Spirit more often, in what parts of life would you experience change?

    _____

    _____

    _____

    _____

    _____

Talking with God

When you pray, go into your room, close the door and pray to your Father, who is unseen. Then your Father, who sees what is done in secret, will reward you. Matthew 6:6 (NIV)

How did Jesus do it? We know *what* Jesus did. He healed lepers. He opened the eyes of the blind. He fed 5000 with only five loaves of bread and two fish. He walked on water. He raised the dead. We know all about *what* Jesus did, but *how* did he do what he did? How did he find the physical strength to deal with the crowds that were constantly pressing in on him? How did he find the wisdom to teach, not to mention standup to the religious leaders who were attacking him and plotting to kill him? How did he find the peace of mind to face his own death?

Of course, many answer the question of "how," by pointing out that Jesus is God. In other words, most believe that he did what he did because he is who he is, God comes in the flesh. And that explanation is certainly accurate, to a degree. At the same time, it fails to appreciate the truth that Jesus was also fully human. Jesus is fully God, but he is also fully human. This means that he had to eat, which means he grew hungry. He had to sleep too, which means he grew tired, even exhausted at times. He had a family, who, it shouldn't be forgotten, doubted his claims to be the Christ for most of his life. He also had friends, who were a blessing in many respects, but like most friendships they were also a burden at times. One of his friends betrayed him to death, and all his friends deserted him when he was arrested.

Luke famously wrote in his gospel that, "Jesus grew in wisdom and stature" (Luke 2:52). The point being that he went through a process of development, just as each of us develop over time. So, when answering the question of *"How* did Jesus do what he did?" we shouldn't dismiss his humanity. What was his secret, humanly speaking? At least part of the answer was prayer. Jesus had a habit of being alone with God.

Mark opens his gospel by noting that "Very early in the morning, while it was still dark, Jesus got up, left the house and went off to a solitary place, where he prayed" (Mark 1:35). The prior evening, the entire town had gathered at the house where Jesus was staying with his disciples, and Jesus had healed many. When the disciples got up the next morning Jesus was gone, and they had to go search for him. When they did finally find him, they pressured him saying, "Everyone is looking for you!" Again, imagine all the pressures that Jesus had to manage daily! It doesn't take much to read between the lines. The disciples were irritated that Jesus was off by himself praying when there are so many people in need.

In Luke's gospel it is simply noted that "Jesus often withdrew to lonely places and prayed" (Luke 5:16). Luke includes it as a matter of fact. This was his regular habit, not just a one off, but a practice that Jesus had of getting alone with God. Later in the gospel of Luke, we learn that on the eve of selecting his twelve disciples that Jesus "spent the night praying to God" (Luke 6:12). On the eve of selecting the men who would be his closest companions for the next three years, and through whom God would establish the Church, Jesus spent the entire night alone with God in prayer. He was doing the same thing the night before he walked on water too (Mark 6:46, John 6:15). And if Jesus needed time alone with the Father, how much more do we need time alone with him?

Within the ancient Jewish faith there were prescribed times for prayer. A devout Jew was to stop and pray at 9:00 a.m., noon, and 3:00 p.m., and they stopped whatever they were doing at those times and prayed, right then and there. Not surprisingly though, some were making sure that they were in public places during these hours, so that they could be seen by others. Jesus noted about them that, "they love to pray standing in the synagogues and on the street corners to be seen by men" (Matthew 6:5). Jesus called them hypocrites, because they were pretending to seek God, but were actually more interested in gaining the admiration of others. And gaining the attention of others was easy to do in the first century, because the posture for prayer at that time was standing, with arms outstretched, palms facing up and head bowed. There was no mistaking what someone is doing in this position.

If Jesus needed time alone with the Father, how much more do we need time alone with him?

Attention seeking easily creeps into our spiritual life. Doesn't it? We can take any good spiritual practice and use it for the wrong purposes, use it to gain the admiration of others or to manipulate others. Jesus gives the prescription for attention seeking though. It's secrecy. When it comes to prayer, good communication with God requires secrecy. We must go into our room, close the door, and meet with God alone, freeing ourselves from the temptation to try and impress others. When we cultivate a secret life with God, we can leave outside the room all the temptations to wear masks, which are meant to impress people. That's where the word "hypocrite" comes from. It comes from a Greek word that means "actor." Actors in ancient Greek plays would often wear various masks, which represented the characters they were portraying. Over time this Greek word came to reference anyone pretending to be other than they are, anyone wearing a mask.

This doesn't mean we can never pray in public. We simply need to make sure that our public prayer life grows out of a private relationship with God. Ultimately, to reap the benefits of these types of practices, we must be motivated by a desire to "be seen by God," and only by God. In the end, Jesus did what Jesus did, at least in part, because of his time alone with God in prayer.

Going Deeper Questions

1. On a scale of 1 to 10, how would you rate the current state of your prayer life? Why did you give yourself that rating?

   _____

   _____

   _____

   _____

2. When and where do you pray? How can you create time and space for secret prayer that allows for undivided attention?

_____

_____

_____

_____

_____

3. What have you experienced as the "reward" of time alone with God? What do you anticipate as the outcome of more alone time with God?

_____

_____

_____

_____

_____

_____

4. Does the directive to cultivate a deeper life of prayer seem like a blessing or a burden?

_____

_____

_____

_____

_____

_____

Our and Us

"This then is how you should pray: 'Our Father in heaven, hallowed be your name.'" Matthew 6:9 (NIV)

If God were to answer our prayers, how many people would be impacted? In other words, how wide is the net of blessings that is cast by our prayers?

As we turn our attention to possibly the most well-known prayer in all of history, take note of the pronouns in this prayer. Do you remember your English grammar lessons? Without a doubt, the nouns in this prayer are important, words like "Father," and "heaven," and "kingdom," and "bread," and "debts" and "evil." The action words are also important, verbs like "give," and "forgive," and "lead," and "deliver." But it's the pronouns that are most often overlooked in the Lord's Prayer, words like "our" and "us."

All the pronouns used within the Lord's Prayer are plural. To be more specific all those referring to the supplicants (i.e., the ones making the requests) are plural. There is not a single singular pronoun in the whole prayer. Not a "me" or an "I" to be found anywhere within the prayer. This means that when Jesus taught his disciples to pray, he taught them to pray as a community and for the community, not simply as individuals.

For example, the prayer starts by recognizing God as "Our" Father, which means the call is for us to praise (i.e., hallow) his name together. In other words, he's not simply my Father, but I have brothers and sisters, with and for whom I'm to be praying.

270

Why does this matter? Someone interested in gaining the applause of men through a public display of prayer can't pray this prayer with any real sincerity (Matthew 6:1-4). And someone who wants to manipulate God for personal gain (Matthew 6:5-8), can't pray this prayer with sincerity either. We simply can't pray for God's kingdom to come, or for his will to be done, if our desire is to serve our own purposes. After all, the point of a kingdom is for the citizens of the kingdom to willingly submit to the Sovereign's rule together, for his glory and everyone's good.

As we work our way deeper into the prayer, we see that we're not simply to be praying for "my" daily bread, but rather that God would give "us," together, "our" daily bread. And it's not just "my" debts for which I should be asking forgiveness, but "our" debts, together. And it's not just "my" temptations that I should be interested in escaping, but Jesus taught us to pray that none of us would fall into temptation. Finally, it's not just "my" deliverance from the evil one for which I should ask, but deliverance for "us" all.

Noting the presence of the plural pronouns changes the entire tone of the prayer. For example, what if praying for the needs of the community is the primary thrust of the Lord's Prayer? What if our prayers are to reflect that we are a part of a kingdom, and that we are following Jesus together? What if, as we pray, we are to be reminded that God is saving a people, not simply individuals, and that Jesus, the groom, will return to claim his bride, not brides.

What if the point of the Lord's Prayer is that God is our Father, not simply my personal Lord and Savior? What if the point is that God is concerned about everyone having daily bread, not simply me? What if the point is that he wants everyone to know the forgiveness of sinful debts, not just me? What if the point is that God wants everyone to know the freedom of forgiving others their sinful debts? What if the point is that temptation is something that befalls a community, and not just something that plagues individuals? What if we are to pray with the recognition that the evil one is targeting us all, and not simply me?

> *Noting the presence of the plural pronouns changes the entire tone of the prayer.*

Even more to the point, might recognizing the weight of plural pronouns in the Lord's Prayer move us to share our daily bread? Might it increase the awareness of the burden that others are carrying because of their debts (i.e. sinful choices)? Might it increase the call for community repentance, as we understand that it is not only individuals, but entire churches and communities that sin against God?

Does this mean that we can never pray for ourselves? No! But the truth is that "we" always includes "me." When I pray with plural pronouns, I am also always praying for myself too. In the end, the good news is that the recognition of plural pronouns in the Lord's Prayer frees us from the selfishness and self-absorption that are so common within prayer.

Going Deeper Questions

1. Considering the Lord's Prayer (Matthew 6:9-15) as a model, what other models of prayer have you found helpful?

   _____

   _____

   _____

   _____

2. How have your prayers been different from or similar to Jesus' prayer?

   _____

   _____

   _____

   _____

3. As you think of the direction from Jesus to pray using plural pronouns, how might this change your prayer life?

   _____

   _____

   _____

   _____

   _____

Spiritual Hunger

"I am the bread of life. Whoever comes to me will never go hungry,
and whoever believes in me will never be thirsty."
John 6:35 (NIV)

Everyone remembers to eat. Even if you're one of those people who can skip breakfast and work straight through lunch, at some point hunger catches up with everyone. We have an unrelenting daily need for food, which is rivaled only by our spiritual hunger. Jesus said, "Man does not live on bread alone, but by every word that proceeds from the mouth of God" (Matthew 4:4). In other words, we have both a physical and spiritual hunger that must be satisfied if we are going to live. Physical hunger is the feeling caused by a body's daily need for nutrients, while spiritual hunger is the feeling caused by a soul's daily need for God's presence.

What's interesting about physical hunger is that there is good reason to believe that it was designed by God as a type of metaphor, by which we might more easily understand our spiritual need for him. For example, there is good reason to believe that Jesus didn't simply adopt the description of himself as the "bread of life" because it is an analogy with which we can all relate, but rather that God designed physical hunger so that we can better understand our spiritual hunger for Jesus. This means rather than thinking that feeding 5000 people with only five loaves of bread was a miracle of convenience, it is more likely that Jesus performed that miracle so that he could teach us that only his presence will satisfy us.

One of the ways that we daily experience God's presence is through prayer. Prayer is an activity of feeding upon God's presence, which means that when we don't pray, it's most often because our souls are feasting on the spiritual equivalent of junk food (e.g. money, sex, achievement, vacations, experiences, possessions, and titles). The richness of our prayer life is directly tied to our recognition that Jesus is the "bread of life." Only Jesus can daily provide our spiritual food. Apart from him we can do nothing (John 15:5), but by him we can do all things (Philippians 4:13).

> *Jesus clearly indicates that one of the ways we will know we long for his presence is in our willingness to give up food for a time in order to seek him in prayer.*

Not surprisingly, if we find ourselves without a desire to pray, or if we lack passion for prayer, the biblical prescription is fasting—that is by going without physical food. Just as God designed physical hunger as a means for reminding us of our spiritual need for his presence, we are directed in Scripture to go without physical food in order to cultivate a greater hunger for God's presence. Going without food, whether it is one meal in a day or a day full of meals, reminds us that we have a desire for God's presence that is greater than even our desire for food. No matter how hungry we may get physically, our spiritual hunger for God's presence is always greater.

When asked why his disciples didn't fast, Jesus answered, "How can the guests of the bridegroom mourn while he is with them? The time will come when the bridegroom will be taken from them; then they will fast" (Matthew 9:15). Jesus explained that fasting is tied to mourning for something lost. While Jesus was present with his disciples there was no reason for them to mourn his absence. But, when he ascended into heaven, his presence was lost to them and then his followers would mourn through fasting. They would fast from food physically, in order to feast on Jesus' presence spiritually.

Jesus clearly indicates that one of the ways we will know we long for his presence is in our willingness to give up food for a time to seek him in prayer. For that reason, every mention of fasting in the Bible is joined to the activity of prayer. For example, the entire church in the city of Antioch fasted together in preparation for sending out missionaries (Acts 13:3) and appointing elders (Acts 14:23). Ezra declared a fast while praying for safety (Ezra 8:23). Nehemiah and Daniel both fasted while praying for God to act on behalf of the Israelites (Nehemiah 1:4, Daniel 9:3). If a hunger for God's presence was measured in the number of meals we missed last month, what would be the total? Or, if a hunger for God's presence was measured in the number of meals we are planning on missing in the month ahead, what would be the total?

Going Deeper Questions

1. How would you describe your current spiritual hunger?

    _____

    _____

    _____

    _____

    _____

    _____

    _____

2. Describe your past experiences with fasting? How have you benefited from spiritually motivated fasting?

    _____

    _____

    _____

    _____

3. How might fasting from food teach you something that you are unable to learn otherwise? Why do you think Jesus assumed we would fast as a part of our spiritual life? (Matthew 4:1-4)

    _____

    _____

    _____

    _____

Through the Church

"His intent was that now, through the church, the manifold wisdom of God should be made known..." Ephesians 3:10 (NIV)

Have you heard the joke about the man stranded on an island? He was alone for years, the only survivor of a shipwreck, when out of the blue another man washed up on the beach. As the two were getting to know one another, the long-time island dweller was excitedly showing the new arrival around, pointing out all the major landmarks. During the tour, the new arrival spotted three huts on a hill far off in the distance. "What are those?" he asked inquisitively. "Oh, that's my village!" answered the longtime island dweller enthusiastically. "Your village?" the new arrival mused, "Why do you need three huts?"

With great pride the man began to explain how the hut on the left was his home, while the hut on the right was his church, and he went into great detail about how he had diligently built both. "Come on, I'll take you up there and you can look around," the longtime island dweller said to the new arrival. "But wait!" the new arrival insisted, "What about the hut in the middle? If the hut on the left is your home and the hut on the right is your church, then for what is the hut in the middle used?" "Oh, well uhh…" the longtime island dweller looked at the ground and stammered. He was obviously made uncomfortable by the question. "Uhh, well, uhh," the longtime island dweller was searching for an explanation when with regret he finally admitted, "That's the church I used to attend."

Relationships within the church can be difficult, and everyone contributes to the difficulty to some degree. However, it will comfort you to know that church was not the idea of any human. It was God's idea and the church was designed by God for a very particular purpose. The purpose of the church is to make known "the manifold wisdom of God." This means that the church is not primarily about us. It involves us and it's meant to be a blessing in our lives, but it is about making God's wisdom known, which was revealed through the sacrifice of Jesus on the cross (Ephesians 3:8-12).

This reality has all types of practical implications for why we come to church, what we expect from the church when we are together, and how we relate to one another within the church. For example, this means that when we come to church, we come not primarily to find friends, or to find a mate, or to make business contacts, or to give our children moral education. The church's purpose is not to make us happy, or to entertain us with programming, or to provide a safe community for our children. Although each of these might very well be by-products of attending church, the primary purpose of the church is to celebrate God's wisdom as revealed in Jesus' life, death and resurrection. You could say that the church is God's vehicle for proclaiming salvation in the world.

When I turned sixteen the only vehicle available for me to drive for some time was my mom's van. Like most American teenage boys, I wished for a truck or a sports car. Anything would have been more masculine than my mom's van. Don't get me wrong. I never refused the van. After all, it was better than walking, but I didn't show much thankfulness for the van either. About the only good word I could say for the van was that it ran, and being a part of the church can feel a lot like driving my mom's van. Maybe we want something faster, something slicker, something sexier, but the church, with all its wrinkles, is what God has provided. In fact, when church becomes popular or slick or sexy, it may not be God's manifold wisdom that is being proclaimed.

One pastor compared the church to Noah's Ark, saying, "The stench inside would be unbearable if it were not for the storm outside."

After all, nothing demonstrates the grace of God as effectively as a group of sinful people celebrating the mercy of God shown toward them in Jesus Christ. Although relationships within the church can be difficult, bearing with one another is a powerful means to displaying the manifold wisdom of God in Jesus. For example, just imagine the sparks that must have flown between Simon the Zealot and Matthew the tax collector, two of Jesus' first disciples. These two men couldn't have been more different. Zealots were a group of Jewish extremists who gave all their effort to establish a nationalist political party for Israel. Zealots wanted the occupying army of Rome kicked out of Israel, and they were committed to this reality even if it required violence. The only people Simon the Zealot would have hated more than the Romans were Jews who collaborated with the Romans—people like tax collectors.

Tax collectors made their living overcharging their fellow Israelites. To make matters even worse, Matthew was a "chief" tax collector, which meant that he was at the top of the tax collector heap. How difficult it must have been for Simon and Mathew to be patient with one another and care for each other?

The longer we are in the church the greater the probability we will wrong someone and be wronged by someone. One pastor compared the church to Noah's Ark, saying, "The stench inside would be unbearable if it were not for the storm outside." By attending church weekly no matter how difficult the relationships are, we proclaim to a watching world that God's grace in Jesus Christ is greater than all our sin.

Going Deeper Questions

1. What has been your experience, both positive and negative, attending church?

   _____
   _____
   _____
   _____
   _____
   _____
   _____
   _____
   _____

2. What have you historically thought to be the purpose of the church?

_____

_____

_____

_____

_____

_____

3. Considering the biblical purpose of the church outlined in Ephesians 3:8-13, how should the programming of the church differ from that of the local park district?

_____

_____

_____

_____

_____

4. Considering the biblical purpose of the church, how should our participation in the church be different from our participation in every other organization on earth?

_____

_____

_____

_____

_____

_____

_____

Fishing and Prayer

For everyone who asks receives; the one who seeks finds; and to the one who knocks, the door will be opened. Luke 11:10 (NIV)

How are you at fishing? Let's be honest. Most people only love the idea of fishing. They love the idea of sitting along the banks of a peaceful lake or river, the sounds of the water near their feet. For this reason, most approach fishing with great anticipation, picturing in their mind's eye the joy-filled surprise of hooking a giant fish and reeling it in. The problem is that the fishing experience often falls far short of what we picture in our minds. Truth be told, catching fish can be difficult. You need to know something about fishing bait, as well as something about the preferred habitat of the fish you are trying to catch. And watching fishing shows, in which good-ole-boys talk about the secrets of fishing, and pull one fish after another out of the water, only seems to increase the probability of disappointment.

So, when I fish, I usually just head out to any body of water and hope that I get lucky. I'm one of those guys who is constantly on the move when fishing, thinking to myself, "Well, maybe the fish are over there." Or, "Maybe over here." And I spend about half of my time moving the boat or walking the shoreline. I'm also one of those guys who is constantly changing bait, wondering if something else on the line might get more attention, and I spend the other half of my time messing with lures, bobbers and slimy things.

Sadly, for many their fishing experience is a whole lot like their experience in prayer. Like with fishing, many love the idea of praying, meeting with God in our secret place and intimately cultivating a relationship with him, but our experience is often much different. It's easy to feel like the answers are out there, but hiding from us, or that we're using the wrong bait and that if we just did something a little different then we might get an answer. Unlike fishing though, getting better at prayer is not a matter of mastering a particular technique, but rather a matter of getting to know our Father. Jesus said, "everyone who asks receives" (Luke 11:10). Can you imagine if everyone who went fishing caught a fish? We pray boldly, with complete confidence, knowing that our Father welcomes us and is eager to answer our prayers. In the New Testament book of Hebrews, we read a similar encouragement.

> *Cast your cares on God and leave them there, at his feet. Don't reel them in constantly. Don't take them back. Cast them upon God boldly because we are the sons and daughters of an infinitely good God.*

> Let us then approach the throne of grace with confidence, so that we may receive mercy and find grace to help us in our time of need. Hebrews 4:16 (NIV)

But in what, or in whom, are we to be confident? Are we to be confident in our ability to pray, or in our Father's desire to care for us? The fishing metaphor applies well here. We can cast our bait with confidence, because in prayer it's not the bait that matters, but our relationship with our Father. We don't have to say the right words, and there are no tricks or techniques to "catching" an answer to our prayers from God. Instead, we are simply encouraged to ask boldly, having the confidence that he always answers. Of course, this is not to say we always get what we want, but simply that God always responds to our prayers. In an attempt to motivate the disciples to pray, Jesus went on to describe to them the character of their Heavenly Father.

> "Which of you fathers, if your son asks for a fish, will give him a snake instead? Or if he asks for an egg, will give him a scorpion? If you then, though you are evil, know how to give good gifts to your children, how much more will your Father in heaven give the Holy Spirit to those who ask him!" Luke 11:11-13 (NIV)

Even if we're unsure about when or how God might answer our prayer, we can always be sure of God's goodness. Jesus is saying that if earthly parents, all of whom struggle with sinfulness, know how to give good gifts to their children, how much more does our Heavenly Father know how to give good gifts to his children. For this reason, Peter encourages us to, "Cast all your cares upon him, because he cares for you" (1 Peter 5:7).

Cast your cares on God and leave them there, at his feet. Don't reel them in constantly. Don't take them back. Cast them upon God boldly because we are the sons and daughters of an infinitely good God. Cast them and then believe fully that he is going to answer because he is a great gift giver. Again, that doesn't mean we will necessarily receive what we have asked for. It does mean that we can live at peace, knowing that the answer we receive is coming from God who is good and who knows what we need before we ask.

Going Deeper Questions

1. How have you historically thought/felt God reacts when he hears your prayers?

   _____

   _____

   _____

   _____

   _____

   _____

   _____

2. Luke 11:5-13 describes both a friend and a father. Compare and contrast these two characters and their attitudes with one another.

   _____

   _____

   _____

   _____

_____

_____

_____

_____

3. How would you describe your posture as you approach God and make petitions? Is it more like the "doubt" described in James 1:5-7 or the "audacity" in Luke 11:8?

_____

_____

_____

_____

_____

_____

4. What are some requests that you feel confident praying about? What are some items that you lack confidence or struggle to voice to God?

_____

_____

_____

_____

_____

_____

_____

_____

_____

Mary Magdalene Matters

Trembling and bewildered, the women went out and fled from the
tomb. They said nothing to anyone, because they were afraid.
Mark 16:8 (NIV)

It's true that believing Jesus was raised from the
dead is a matter of faith. We must believe without seeing
Jesus ourselves. At the same time, it is completely
reasonable to believe the accounts of Scripture are eye-
witness reports. It's reasonable to believe the reports of
Scripture because the gospel writers included people like
Mary Magdalene in the story.

Most-likely born and raised in the city of Magdala,
which was located along the western shores of the Sea of
Galilee, Mary probably met Jesus as he made his way from
town to town teaching and healing people. Magdala was
only three miles from Jesus' home in Capernaum, and like
so many others Mary probably went to see Jesus as he
came through Magdala, wanting to hear first-hand this
famous rabbi's teaching and see for herself if the reports
of his miraculous powers were true. But, unlike so many
other people, Mary had an acute need. She had seven
demons that were tormenting her (Luke 8:1-3).

Mary was debilitated physically and mentally and
emotionally by demonic presence, which is not to say that
everyone who suffers in these ways has a demon. That's
not what the Bible teaches. The Bible does teach though
that everyone who has a demon, especially seven, is
debilitated physically, emotionally, and mentally.

That all changed for Mary when Jesus healed her. Mary was set free from evil. Once in bondage she was released and restored, and she followed Jesus from town to town and supported his ministry financially. In fact, Mary Magdalene was one of the few who followed Jesus to the bitter end. Three of the four gospels place her at the foot of the cross. There she remained until Jesus' body was taken down from the cross and laid in a tomb. Moreover, all four of the gospels name Mary Magdalene as the first person to visit Jesus' tomb on resurrection morning (Mark 16:1-8).

Mary Magdalene had experienced the power of Jesus! She was delivered from seven demons, which had wreaked havoc on her mind and body. She had also followed Jesus for the better part of three years, sitting under his teachings and seeing his miracles firsthand, even supporting his ministry from her own finances. And she was one of the few who had the courage to attend the crucifixion. Yet, Mark records that "trembling and bewildered," all the women fled from the tomb, and "they said nothing to anyone, because they were afraid" (Mark 16:8).

Why do you suppose that was Mary's response? Of all the people who should have been anything but bewildered and afraid, it was Mary Magdalene. Yet, Mark reports that one of Jesus' closest and most committed followers responded to the news of his resurrection in stunned silence and fearful disobedience to the angel's explicit instructions to tell others. What are we to make of this?

I don't know why Mary responded like that. But what I do know is that Mark's report of Mary's reaction strikes me as a most accurate presentation of what is a very common response to the news of Jesus being raised from the dead. Disbelief. It can be hard to believe that Jesus was raised from the dead. Even those closest and most committed to Jesus wrestled to believe, at first.

Now, if you are thinking, "Ok, but don't you want to convince me to believe, rather than comfort me in my doubting?" Yes. But a part of believing requires engaging our minds. Faith, believing in something we haven't seen, and facts are not in competition, but are complementary realities, and there is good reason to believe that the accounts of the resurrection are in fact eye-witness testimony.

Here's why. If, as a first-century author, you wanted to write the most convincing proof of Jesus' resurrection, how would you have gone about it? If you were Matthew, or Mark, or Luke or John, how would you have composed the story? I can tell you how you would not have gone about it. You would not have mentioned that women were the first to discover the tomb was empty. In our modern world, we think nothing of the fact that women were first on the scene and discovered the tomb was empty, and rightly so. But in the ancient world, the testimony of women was not trusted. The testimony of a woman was not even admissible as evidence in a court of law in the first century. Women didn't have enough social or cultural capital to merit a hearing. Yet, each gospel reports that women were the first to discover that the tomb was empty.

Why does this matter? It matters because it means that when we read the resurrection accounts, we are not reading the attempts of first-century authors to make the story believable. Instead, we are reading eye-witness accounts of a most believable report. And to make the resurrection accounts even more believable, John reports in his gospel, that a very specific woman, that is someone who had been physically ill, emotionally unstable and mentally insane for much of her life, was the first person to see and speak with Jesus after he was raised (John 20:11-18). Again, this tells us that the Gospel authors didn't massage the story to make it more palatable for their audience. They didn't edit the facts. They simply reported them.

In the first century world, in which women were basically treated as property, how easy would it have been for the gospel writers to feel pressure to massage the details of resurrection morning? How much more "believable" would it have been if someone famous or powerful had been the first person to discover the tomb empty. But that is not what the authors of the Gospels did. Instead, they simply reported the facts.

Like Mary we are all broken and in need of healing. Admittedly, the extent of Mary Magdalene's brokenness was unique, but the cause of her brokenness is shared among all humanity. Sin is shared among all humanity and the consequences are felt by all, namely disease and death. That's why the resurrection is needed. Truth be told, Mary was most likely first at the tomb that morning because she was keenly aware of all that Jesus had done for her.

Going Deeper Questions

1. What doubts have you overcome regarding Jesus' resurrection, and what doubts still linger?

   _____

   _____

   _____

   _____

   _____

   _____

2. How does the outcome of Mary Magdalene's story affect your approach to doubt, whether your own or somebody else's?

   _____

   _____

   _____

   _____

   _____

3. Based on Mary's story and other scripture, how do you think God feels about doubt? As a community, how can we better reflect God's posture towards doubt?

   _____

   _____

   _____

   _____

   _____

Typology

The blood will be a sign for you on the houses where you are, and when I see the blood, I will pass over you. No destructive plague will touch you when I strike Egypt. Exodus 12:13 (NIV)

Typology is the practice of seeing events in the Old Testament as examples, or patterns, of what is later revealed in the New Testament. While typology certainly has its limits, identifying types began with the New Testament authors. Paul saw Jesus as a type of Adam, but without sin (Romans 5:14). In the book of Hebrews, much of the Tabernacle and Temple is described as a type of the ministry experienced by faith in Jesus. And one of the most vivid of types is seen in the Passover.

For example, John the Baptist famously declared, when he saw Jesus for the first time, "Behold the Lamb of God" (John 1:29). And it was the Passover meal that Jesus was celebrating with his disciples on the eve of his crucifixion, at which time he drew parallels between the body and blood of the Passover lamb, which they were eating, and his own death on the cross. And in the book of Revelation, John called Jesus "the Lamb of God" (Revelation 13:8). Passover was instituted during the tenth plague. Moses had been pleading with Pharaoh for the Israelites' release, but nothing would soften Pharaoh's heart. Frogs, gnats, flies, boils, hail, and locusts all came, but nothing rattled Pharaoh. In the tenth and final plague though, the firstborn in Egypt died, and only those who marked the door of their home with lamb's blood survived (Exodus 12:6-11).

In other words, in every house in Egypt blood was shed, either the blood of the first born in that household or the blood of an innocent lamb. God's judgement was coming, and some would be protected and some would be punished, and the difference was based solely upon those who willingly received God's provision of a mark of lamb's blood on their house. Of course, even today we know that judgement is coming upon the whole earth because of sin, and eternal punishment is awaiting those who do not receive the mark of the blood of God's Lamb, Jesus Christ (John 3:18, John 16:11).

If you are unfamiliar with the Old Testament Passover, the lamb would have most likely been killed in the doorway of each Israelite home. We learn from later accounts that the head of the household would have used hyssop to apply the spilled blood of the lamb to the door frame of the household. Hyssop is a small bushy plant which was often used in purification rights. David said in repentance, "Purge me with hyssop, and I shall be clean" (Psalm 51:7).

Taking hyssop, the father of the household dipped the branch in blood and touched it to the top of the door, and then he would smear some on the two side posts of the door frame. There would have been blood at the foot of the door, where the lamb was slain, the head of the door and both sides. It doesn't take much imagination to see the cross of Jesus in this pattern. Jesus' feet were bloodied with a spike driven through them, his head was bloodied with a crown of thorns pressed into his skull, and his hands bloodied with nails fastening him to the crossbeam.

Christians are those who have marked the doors of their souls, so to speak, with the Blood of the lamb. But what does it mean that Jesus is our Passover Lamb (1 Corinthians 5:7)? Moses explained that:

> When the LORD goes through the land to strike down the Egyptians, he will see the blood on the top and sides of the doorframe and will pass over that doorway, and he will not permit the destroyer to enter your houses and strike you down. Exodus 12:23 (NIV)

Note that a separate third party is doing the killing. While it is true that God is sovereign and nothing happens without his permission, God did not kill the children of Egypt. A "destroyer" is executing judgment, not God. This was most likely an angelic being. God, though, is doing something very different than the destroyer. God is "passing over" the Israelite homes, all those marked with blood. What does this mean? The Hebrew word for Passover is *pesah*. This noun is derived from a verb form that is used only five times in the Hebrew Bible, and it *always* denotes a sheltering action. In fact, Passover most accurately means "cover over." In other words, Passover does not denote God's passing by the Israelite houses, as we think of passing someone on the highway in our car. Instead, God was establishing a deterrent at the houses marked with blood, sheltering the Israelite families by stationing himself immovably at their doors in order to protect them against the destroyer. Do you see the difference? God is not doing the killing in this passage.

God is doing the protecting, and it's the blood of the lamb that draws God's protection. The good news of the gospel is that God hovers over all those who receive Jesus' sacrifice on their behalf, protecting them from the destroyer of death because of sinfulness.

Going Deeper Questions

1. How have you historically understood God's role in the death of the Egyptians during the tenth plague, as well as in the saving of the Israelites?

   _____

   _____

   _____

   _____

2. What might be God's purposes in providing us with "types," or patterns, in his work of redemption?

   _____

   _____

   _____

   _____

3. Considering Isaiah 31:5, how is this imagery helpful in understanding God's care of his people?

   _____

   _____

   _____

   _____

A Theology of Singing

Let the message of Christ dwell among you richly as you teach and admonish one another with all wisdom through psalms, hymns, and songs from the Spirit, singing to God with gratitude in your hearts.
Colossians 3:16 (NIV)

When my oldest was looking at colleges, we visited the Naval Academy. The military lifestyle is one to which I had never been exposed, and it was quite impressive. I came away feeling that our country is protected by men and women who are passionate about their jobs and excellent at what they do. One of the experiences that most marked me during the visit was hearing the Midshipmen sing together. They sang loudly and with conviction.

Do you know why soldiers sing? Do you realize that all armies throughout history have sung together? It's fairly straightforward. Singing strengthens one's hope and resolve in difficult times. Singing together reminds us of why we fight, as well as for whom and/or for what we fight. Singing is powerful, unifying and motivating.

Soon after visiting the Naval Academy, I watched online the 2014 Commencement Address given by Naval Admiral William McRaven at the University of Texas. Millions have watched his speech on YouTube. In the speech the Admiral described what he learned during Naval Seal training, and one of the stories he tells is of "Hell Week," which comes in the ninth week of training. During "Hell Week" the Naval trainers work the hardest to force the seal recruits to quit, to give up, to drop out.

"Hell Week" includes six days with virtually no sleep, constant marching and persistent heckling, as the recruits are pressed to the very edge. McRaven said it was the Wednesday of Hell Week, after marching for 15 hours into the middle of the night, that they found themselves neck deep in mud, where they were ordered to stay for eight hours, until the sun came up. The trainers taunted them, reminding them that the torture would end if only five of the recruits would quit, and give up on being a Navy Seal.

When the taunting and heckling was at its worst though, McRaven said that the recruits started singing, and it was singing that carried them through the night. Singing gave them hope. Even though their trainers ordered them to stop singing and threatened to make them stay longer in the mud if they continued to sing, the recruits continued to sing loudly. McRaven concluded his speech by insisting it was singing together that got them through that ordeal. He said, "If you want to change the world, start singing when you are up to your neck in mud."

The Apostle Paul wrote of the power and importance of singing to one another. He wrote:

> Let the message of Christ dwell among you richly as you teach and admonish one another with all wisdom through psalms, hymns, and songs from the Spirit, singing to God with gratitude in your hearts. Colossians 3:16 (NIV)

We know what it means to teach one another. It means to give instruction. Although we are less familiar with the word "admonish," it simply means to correct one another. This teaching and admonishing is to be done with "all wisdom," which means simply that it is to be done with understanding and discernment. But "how" is it to be done? It is to be done by singing to one another! It is to be done through "psalms, hymns, and songs from the Spirit, singing to God with gratitude in your hearts."

Unfortunately, too many folks see singing in church as a placeholder until the preacher gets up to teach and admonish the congregation. Others, often view singing as something in which only the musically gifted are to participate. According to Paul though, singing is a primary means for teaching and admonishing one another. Through singing to one another the message of Christ dwells more richly among us.

> *A life of song is a direct byproduct of the Spirit's filling and controlling our lives.*

Is singing our only opportunity for teaching and admonishing? In other words, should we do away with preaching altogether and only sing to one another? No! But singing is to have a central place in the gathering of God's people, in that it is a biblical directed method of teaching and admonishing one another. Through singing together we effectively preach to one another the message of Christ. Truth be told, there should never be only one preacher in a church. Every member preaches each time they sing together, which enriches the message of Christ among his people.

It shouldn't surprise us that singing is to play such a key role in the life of the church, especially as we learn that there were singers in the ancient Temple, men whose roles were to do nothing but lead in song (Nehemiah 11:22). It shouldn't surprise us that singing is to play such a key role in the life of the church in that God himself sings over us as a "Mighty Warrior" (Zephaniah 3:17). And it shouldn't surprise us that singing is to play such a key role in the life of the church when we remember that songs are sung around the clock before the throne of God (Revelation 4:8). Finally, it shouldn't surprise us that singing is a direct result of the Spirit's presence in our lives. As we allow more of the Spirit's leadership in our lives, we will become people of song; "Then you will sing psalms and hymns and make music in your heart to the Lord" (Ephesians 5:18-19). A life of song is a direct byproduct of the Spirit's filling and controlling our lives.

Going Deeper Questions

1. Considering the following descriptions, which best represents your posture toward singing in worship? (eagerly, willingly, dutifully, reluctantly) Share with others why this word best describes your posture toward singing.

   _____

   _____

   _____

   _____

_____

_____

_____

_____

_____

_____

_____

2. What would need to happen for you to strengthen your habit of singing when gathered with God's people?

_____

_____

_____

_____

_____

3. How does your church do at preaching together through song, and how might the church strengthen this activity?

_____

_____

_____

_____

_____

_____

Monopoly

It is hard for a rich man to enter the kingdom of heaven.
Again I tell you, it is easier for a camel to go through the eye of a
needle than for a rich man to enter the kingdom of God.
Matthew 19:23-24 (NIV)

Since the game's creation in 1933, Monopoly has sold an estimated 250 million game boards. Over one billion folks have played the game, and it's been published in 47 languages and sold in over 100 countries. If you're one of the many who has played the game, and lost, then you've probably experienced what the social psychologist Paul Piff describes as "self-focus." Piff, a professor of psychology and social behavior, focuses his research on how wealth impacts interpersonal relationships. One of his studies includes rigged games of Monopoly, in order to observe the relational strain between players caused by wealth inequality. His findings are fascinating, and if you've ever lost at Monopoly your experience will probably confirm some of his findings.

Piff found that Monopoly winners, even in rigged games, tend to: 1) believe they deserve their winning position, 2) cheat more than their losing opponents, in order to insure or preserve their winning position, and 3) suffer from a diminished sense of compassion toward their opponents, which is witnessed in activities such as gloating. If you are thinking, "Well, of course Monopoly winners behave poorly, but no one really behaves that way in real life." You're wrong. The truth is that people behave even worse in real life.

In parallel studies, Piff found that the driving habits of those with expensive cars are much worse than those with less expensive cars. There is apparently a direct correlation between the cost of one's car and one's "self-focused" behavior. In fact, the more expensive one's car, the more likely the driver is to 1) believe they are entitled to certain privileges on the road, 2) break the law, in order to preserve their advantages, and 3) show little compassion for others on the road. In another parallel study, Piff found that the wealthier an individual the more likely they were to take candy from a bowl marked "for children only." In fact, Piff found that the wealthy cheat twice as much as the poor, and the wealthy are 44% less likely to share their resources than the poor. To summarize Piff's findings, increased wealth and status in society lead to increased self-focus and, in turn, decreased compassion, altruism, and ethical behavior.

If this is shocking news, Jesus said something eerily similar. Jesus said that having wealth makes it difficult to get into heaven. He said, "It is easier for a camel to go through the eye of a needle than for a rich man to enter the kingdom of God" (Matthew 19:24). Why is it so hard for rich folks to get into heaven? Because we're tempted to make ourselves the focus of life, just as Piff learned, rather than follow after Jesus and live lives of generosity and compassion. While this reality may feel threatening, there is a ray of hope. If you've noticed increasingly "self-focused" behavior in your life, or if you've wrestled with showing compassion towards those with fewer resources, there is good news. According to the Bible, the wealthy are not necessarily doomed to Hell.

Do you remember the story of Zacchaeus? He was a "chief tax collector" and very wealthy (Luke 19:1-10). Yet, Zacchaeus escaped from his self-focused lifestyle and received salvation. Tax collectors made their living by collecting more tax than was required by the Roman government. Whatever they could collect beyond what the Romans required, was theirs to keep. Being a chief tax collector meant that Zacchaeus was exceptional at extorting money. Remember, Israel was an occupied territory at that time, and Rome had a habit of employing Israelites to collect the taxes, which meant that Zacchaeus was not only extorting money from people in general, but that he was gauging his own countrymen. He was helping Rome continue to oppress Israel, and growing wealthy in the process.

Yet, Zacchaeus was so moved by having Jesus in his house that he offered to give half all his possessions to the poor and pay back four times the amount he had stolen from others. Bear in mind that the Jewish Law defined generosity as giving away 20% to the poor, while Zacchaeus committed to give half of his wealth to the poor. Furthermore, according to the law only two times the damages was required, when someone had stolen from another person (Leviticus 5:16, Numbers 5:7). Yet, Zacchaeus promised to repay four times all that he had stolen. In response to Zacchaeus' change of heart Jesus declared, "Today salvation has come to this house."

Of course, we know that salvation is only and always a result of receiving God's grace. Salvation is not something we can earn, but is something we receive as a gift out of the kindness of God's heart (Ephesians 2:8-9).

This means that Zacchaeus must have met with God's grace when Jesus entered his home. All too familiar with his sinfulness, God's grace was greater than Zacchaeus' greed. Greed opposes God's character and purposes in the world, because it makes us the center of the universe. Greed takes God off the throne, so to speak, and puts us on the throne. But, the good news is that God's grace can change our greed, in that it shows us that we are loved despite making ourselves the center of the universe. When Jesus entered his life, Zacchaeus could no longer believe that he was the center of all things, or that more money would provide him with what he was wanting in life. When Jesus entered his life, he became keenly aware of the emptiness in his greedy behaviors, as well as the fullness of following Jesus.

Does this mean that we each need to give half of our possessions away to the poor? No. Following Jesus is not that formulaic. Remember, Jesus is alive, and he calls each of his followers to listen to his voice and do as he tells us to do. Zacchaeus' story does mean though that while I can't tell you how much to give away financially, I can tell you that God will lead all those who have received his grace toward generosity.

Going Deeper Questions

1. How were you moved in hearing about the different attitudes and actions of the wealthy?

   _____

   _____

   _____

_____

_____

_____

2. Reading Zacchaeus' story, try to articulate the grace he received from Jesus and how that may have felt (Luke 19:1-10).

_____

_____

_____

_____

_____

3. Do you think you've experienced those same elements of grace from Jesus? How have they affected your life?

_____

_____

_____

_____

_____

4. In what ways can you show the same type of grace that Jesus shared with Zacchaeus, with the people around you? Name a specific person that you could show grace to in the upcoming weeks?

_____

_____

_____

_____

_____

A Tale Of Two Thieves

Then he said, "Jesus, remember me when you come into your kingdom." Jesus answered him, "Truly I tell you, today you will be with me in paradise." Luke 23:42-43 (NIV)

In 2014 I traveled with a friend to the Danville State Correctional Facility. A ministry conference was being held inside the prison, and several pastors had been invited to preach. Danville State Prison has a full seminary and inmates can earn a Master's in Divinity degree while behind bars. Each year the seminary hosts a preaching conference, and it was for me an experience of power that I had not previously known.

Every issue imaginable is present in the lives of prison inmates. Yet, I'll never forget singing with the inmates before I was to get up and preach. They sang with tremendous passion and deep conviction. In fact, many of the inmates appeared to be freer in their expression of love for God in ways that those who are physically free and sing weekly in churches are not. At the same time, there is a longstanding debate in the correctional world about whether criminals can really be changed. But make no mistake. The clear message of the gospel is that no one is too hardened by sin's deceitfulness that they cannot be changed. The thief who hung next to Jesus on a cross is the quintessential example. He was changed dramatically and eternally. According to Scripture, no one is too addicted, or too angry, or too cynical, or too selfish that they can't be changed by faith in Jesus.

At the same time, it's interesting to note that neither the gospel of Matthew nor the gospel of Mark report that one of the two criminals crucified beside Jesus was changed. Matthew and Mark report that *both* criminals who were crucified with Jesus ridiculed him (Matthew 27:39, Mark 15:32). Yet, only Luke reports that one of the two criminals was changed, actually defending Jesus and asking to be "remembered" by Jesus when he came into his "kingdom" (Luke 23:43). What are we to make of this?

Of course, some make this a contradiction, and claim that the gospels are unreliable. However, it is just as reasonable to conclude that both criminals ridiculed Jesus for some period of time, as Matthew and Mark report, but that one of the two criminals was changed, as Luke reports. In other words, Matthew and Mark's and Luke's accounts need not be understood as contradictory. In fact, all three accounts are easily harmonized, as it is entirely possible that one moment both criminals were ridiculing Jesus, and the next moment one of the criminals began defending Jesus. That, after all, is the nature of spiritual change, turning from sinful behavior.

> *Make no mistake though, the clear message of the gospel is that no one is too hardened by sin's deceitfulness that they cannot be changed.*

What's more troubling for me than these differences in the gospel accounts, is the reality that only one criminal changed. After all, if these two criminals both witnessed the same things, then why weren't they either both changed or both remain unchanged? While Luke doesn't seem to present an answer to this question, there is some comfort to be had in Luke's gospel. Throughout Luke's gospel he offers stories that present spiritual dichotomies, and the account of one repentant and one unrepentant criminal fits this pattern.

For example, there are two birth announcements in Luke's gospel, one given to Zechariah and one to Mary, Joseph's fiancé (Luke 1). There are also the stories of two sisters, Martha who was distracted by all that worried her and Mary who sat contentedly at Jesus' feet learning (Luke 10). There are also the stories of two men who go to the Temple to pray, one arrogant, who is not heard by God, and one humble, who is answered by God (Luke 18). Finally, there are the stories of two criminals crucified with Jesus, one unrepentant and one repentant (Luke 23).

In each of these cases, Luke presents dichotomies of faith. By telling these parallel stories, Luke helps us to frame matters of faith, forcing us to ask whether we will be full of faith like Mary, the fiancé of Joseph, or focused on Jesus like Mary, the sister of Martha, or humble, like the man who prayed in the Temple. While Luke doesn't explain why only one criminal was changed, it appears that he offers the story of these two criminals so that we will wrestle with whether we will be repentant or unrepentant.

Going Deeper Questions

1. What differences do you see in how the two thieves interacted with Jesus? (Luke 23:32-43) What elements of repentance are evident, and what elements of unrepentance are evident?

_____

_____

_____

_____

_____

2. What are common barriers to repentance, and how might they be overcome?

_____

_____

_____

_____

_____

3. How would your interactions with people change if you knew they would never accept Christ? How would they change if you knew they eventually would accept Christ?

_____

_____

_____

_____

_____

Choosing Friends Wisely

You adulterous people, don't you know that friendship with the world is hatred toward God? Anyone who chooses to be a friend of the world becomes an enemy of God. James 4:4 (NIV)

His name was Demas and he was a traveling companion of Paul. For this reason, in several places, when the team members are listed, Demas is positioned prominently in the list. For example, Paul closes the little New Testament book of Philemon writing, "Epaphras, my fellow prisoner greets you, as do Mark, Aristarchus, Demas, and Luke, my fellow laborers" (Philemon 24). Paul also mentions Demas in his close to the book of Colossians, saying that Luke and Demas send their greetings (Colossians 4:14)!

While we don't know a lot more about Demas other than that he was a close friend of Paul, someone who accompanied Paul on his missionary journeys, even suffering hardships with Paul at times, we do know that somewhere along the way he took a wrong turn. Sometime around 67 AD, about 34 years after Jesus was raised from the grave, Demas abandoned the faith. We know this because Paul wrote about it in his second letter to Timothy saying:

> Do your best to come to me quickly, for Demas, because he loved this world, has deserted me and has gone to Thessalonica. 2 Timothy 4:10 (NIV)

Isn't that sad? We know that Paul wrote his second letter to Timothy from a Roman prison, just before he was martyred for his faith, which means that Demas most likely deserted Paul, while he was in prison, abandoning him in his time of greatest need. Moreover, it is clear from Paul's description that Demas not only abandoned his friendship with Paul, but also the ministry and his faith, because he "loved this world."

While Paul doesn't give us a specific description of what Demas loved *about* the world, Demas' story should challenge each of us, because a love of the world can draw us away from God. While we know that God loves the people of the world (John 3:16), what about "friendship with the world" makes us an "enemy of God"? The disciple John offers a description of the dangers to our faith that exist in the world. He wrote:

> If anyone loves the world, the love of the Father is not in him. For everything in the world—the cravings of sinful man, the lust of the eyes and the boasting of what he has and does—comes not from the Father but from the world. 1 John 2:15-16 (NIV)

To befriend the world is to allow our cravings to rule our lives—the lust of the eyes, the lust of the flesh and the boastful pride of life. What was it that drew Demas away? Hard to know. But each day we are faced with many choices that involve deciding whether we will love God or the world. For example:

- Will we buy a smaller house than we can afford to give more to God's work, or will we squeeze into a mortgage that will prevent our giving generously?
- Will we be the same in private that we are in public, or will we only pursue godliness when it can win the admiration of others?
- Will we edit our speech concerned about what co-workers and neighbors may think, or will we speak unashamedly about the gospel?
- Will we fill our souls with consuming and purchasing, or will we be filled by the Holy Spirit?

The Apostle Peter wrote that we are to live as strangers and aliens in this world (1 Peter 2:11-12), because this world is not our home. Eugene Petersen translated the same verses as "Friends, this world is not your home, so don't make yourselves cozy in it" (The Message). You can tell when growing cozy in this world is not someone's goal, because their actions will strike the people who are making this world their home as strange. Godliness is so dramatically different than the world's method of operation, that the way we lead our lives will appear strange to those who are friends with the world.

It's interesting to note that first-century Christians were generally labeled as atheists and attacked because they rejected the objects of pagan worship. They would no longer go to the pagan temples and sleep with the shrine prostitutes, or bow to the idols in the temple, which unnerved their neighbors! Apart from accepting our status as strangers in this world, we cannot grow spiritually. Which doesn't mean we can't enjoy life and the blessings of the Lord, it simply means that we can't live for this life. We will either be friends with God, or friends with the world.

Going Deeper Questions

1. How have you been perceived as "strange" by those who are a part of the world?

_____

_____

_____

_____

_____

2. What about "the world" do you find attractive? What part/s of the world are you tempted to love?

_____

_____

_____

_____

_____

3. How do you actively avoid the temptations to befriend the world?

_____

_____

_____

_____

_____

Storm Stories

Everyone who hears these words of mine and puts them
into practice is like a wise man who built his house
on the rock. Matthew 7:24 (NIV)

PBS produced a four-hour television special titled "The Question of God." The series was based on a book with the same name, which was written by a Harvard professor named Dr. Armand Nicholi. The book's content, and the content of the PBS special, are based on a course that Dr. Nicholi taught at Harvard for over 25 years. It's a course that compares the lives of Sigmund Freud and C.S. Lewis.

Why compare these two men's lives? According to Dr. Nicholi, these two men are the most influential philosophers of our modern world. At the same time, he says you couldn't find two more diametrically opposed perspectives on life. Freud was an atheist and a materialist, which means he believed that there is no God and that the material world is all there is to our existence (i.e. nothing beyond our physical reality). For this reason, Freud built his philosophy on what he called the "pleasure principle" and suggested that sexual expression was the greatest goal of life and sexual repression was the greatest enemy of humanity. The highest and only expression of love for Freud came through sexual experience. Of course, his philosophy was a driving force in the sexual revolution of the 1960's, and it is easy to see how many in our culture today continue to embrace this philosophy.

Lewis, on the other hand, was a theist (i.e. a believer in God) and a follower of Jesus, which meant he tried to "put into practice" all that Jesus taught, including disciplined living and sexual restraint. For Lewis the highest expression of love came through self-sacrifice, not sexual expression, and self-sacrifice is best seen in Jesus's sacrificial death on the cross.

What is most fascinating about Dr. Nicholi's book, as well as the PBS series, is that it traces the personal outcome of these men's philosophies in their own lives. Everyone agrees that these men were brilliant, but the book makes clear the outcomes of their philosophies. The fact of the matter is that Freud was miserable much of his life, even taking his own life in the end, with the help of a physician friend, while Lewis found great joy and deep meaning through his relationship with God and others. About

> *Wisdom though, is far more than simply knowing what to do. Wisdom is acting on what we know to be true, putting into practice what we have been taught.*

following him, Jesus said, "Everyone who hears these words of mine and puts them into practice is like a wise man who built his house on the rock" (Matthew 7:24). Dr. Nicholi's goal, unapologetically, is to point out the foolishness of Freud's life and the wisdom of Lewis' life as a follower of Jesus.

In the hot climate of the Middle East the soil is baked and hard because of the intense heat, and all lots appear to be equally suitable for a building site. However, in the winter months, sudden and heavy rainfall, along with stiff winds, create rivers of mud that sweep through valleys carrying off everything that is not securely built upon a bedrock. This means that a builder must take extra care in this type of climate to dig down to the rock beneath the dirt, excavating the loose sand and establishing the foundation upon an immovable object, so that when the storms of life come he doesn't have to fear or worry. Jesus' point was that when the storms of life come those who built their life upon his teaching will endure, while those who didn't will suffer loss. Here's a short summary of some of Jesus' teachings.

- Seek reconciliation quickly (Matthew 5:23-26)
- Avoid temptation (Matthew 5:27-30)
- Keep your word (Matthew 5:33-37)
- Forgive when insulted (Matthew 5:39)
- Mend relationships eagerly (Matthew 5:40)
- Serve sacrificially (Matthew 5:41)
- Give generously (Matthew 5:42)
- Love your enemies (Matthew 5:43-48)
- Live humbly (Matthew 6:1-6)
- Invest in eternity (Matthew 6:19-24)
- Don't judge others (Matthew 7:1-6)
- Pray diligently (Matthew 7:7-11)
- Treat others kindly (Matthew 7:12).

I'm a big fan of the Weather Channel. I can sit and watch their feature segments titled "Storm Stories" for hours. For some reason though every storm story seems to include a couple of people who against better judgment tried to drive their car through high water only to nearly lose their lives, and it makes for great television. There isn't a licensed driver who doesn't know better than to drive through deep water during a torrential rain, yet for some reason people constantly do it.

Wisdom though, is far more than simply knowing what to do. Wisdom is acting on what we know to be true, putting into practice what we have been taught. After all, everyone faces storms, both the wise and the foolish. Storms are no respecters of people. Following Jesus is not a strategy for avoiding storms. C.S. Lewis faced as many trying circumstances in his life as Sigmund Freud. The promise is not that those who follow after Jesus' teachings will be spared trials. The promise of this passage is that a life wisely founded upon the teachings of Jesus will endure the storms of life.

Why do Jesus' teachings uniquely enable us to endure the storms of life? Can't the same be said of Buddha, or Mohammed, or Moses? The answer is that Jesus is uniquely qualified to help us endure storms because Jesus overcame the greatest storm of all, namely death. It's the resurrection of Jesus that makes Jesus unique as a teacher. He alone is qualified to guarantee life in the face of death, because he alone overcame death. Jesus' teachings are wise, but the power of his teachings ultimately hinges on Jesus' victory over death. After all, true wisdom is to not only embrace the teachings of Jesus, but the person and work of Jesus, his life and death and resurrection. That is what enables us to endure the greatest storms of life.

Going Deeper Questions

1. What storms have you endured in life?

   _____

   _____

   _____

   _____

   _____

   _____

2. How did Jesus' teachings help you through the storms you have faced?

   _____

   _____

   _____

   _____

   _____

3. How might you better prepare for storms coming in the future?

   _____

   _____

   _____

   _____

   _____

FOLLOWING JESUS
Defining Discipleship in the 21st Century

People have lots of questions about what it means to follow Jesus, but very little time. *Following Jesus* provides answers for those on the go. Whether you are a non-Christian, wanting to better understand the Christian faith, or a Christian wanting to succinct definition of discipleship, this book is for you.

In that first-century world disciples were those who detached themselves from their own way of life and reattached themselves to a *rabbi* (teacher), committing themselves to his service and to becoming like him in every way. When following a rabbi, first-century disciples would pay attention to every word he spoke and every move he made, sometimes even trying to mimic his mannerisms. So complete was a disciple's commitment to the rabbi that it became the defining element of their character, and the nature of what it means to be a disciple has not changed in over 2000 years.

Following Jesus is aimed at defining discipleship in order to help those following after Jesus better understand his call upon their lives.

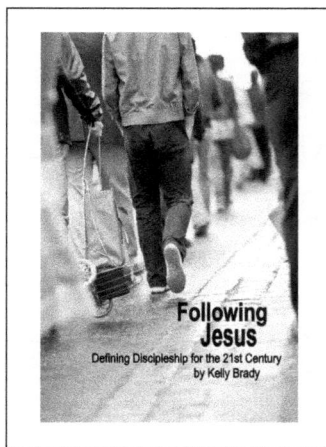

Following Jesus
Defining Discipleship for the 21st Century
by Kelly Brady

DRIVE THRU THEOLOGY
A guide to the Bible's teaching for those on the go

People have lots of questions about what the Bible teaches, but very little time. This book provides quick answers for those on the go. Offering concise theological statements on a broad range of topics, this book is meant to be a quick reference guide. Sprinkled throughout are also short answers to commonly asked questions about Christian faith. Questions like: "How much faith is needed to receive healing?" and "Why might our prayers go unanswered?" As a pastor, I am reminded daily that shepherds do not grow the grass. Shepherds simply point to where they can find the grass. This means anytime we are caring for others spiritually, our job is to simply point to the truth found in Scripture. Our job is not to try and create food, but rather direct them to the nourishment of Scripture. Ultimately, it is only the truth of God's Word that sustains God's people.

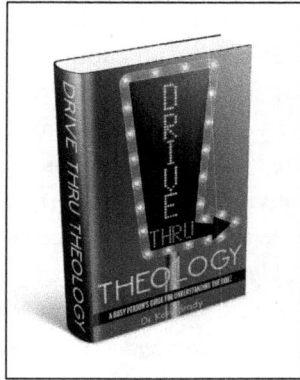

It is tempting to offer our own wisdom when guiding others spiritually, or the popular psychology of the day. But the greatest need we have is to hear the truth of God's Word, because it is the Scripture that is "God-breathed" (2 Timothy 3:16).

SHEPHERDING
The Elder Notebook of Glen Ellyn Bible Church

The Apostle Paul appointed Elders in each church he established (Acts 14:23), and he wrote that serving as an Elder is a noble task (1 Timothy 3:1). In fact, having a desire to serve as an Elder is one of the first qualifications for service. In an effort to strengthen the office of Elder at GEBC and equip the men who have a desire for service, we have put together this notebook.

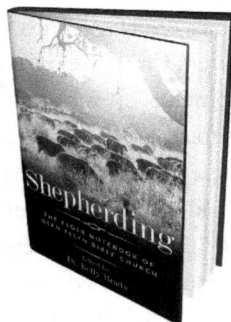

Shepherding is the product of a community effort, as both the Elders and the staff of Glen Ellyn Bible Church have contributed countless hours in research, prayer and study to provide this written record of our theology and philosophy of ministry. It is our desire is to strengthen not only the people of GEBC by providing competent and godly leadership, but to share what we've learned with other churches in order to advance God's Kingdom around the world. Toward that end, you are free to reproduce any portion of this notebook for educational purposes, provided you do not change the content or charge others for the content. Finally, proceeds from the sale of this book go to the Benevolence Fund of Glen Ellyn Bible Church, which is dedicated to meeting the needs of physically and spiritually impoverished.

www.ingramcontent.com/pod-product-compliance
Lightning Source LLC
Chambersburg PA
CBHW060456090426
42735CB00011B/2003